SIP & FEAST

FAMILY FAVORITE RECIPES

From Our Kitchen to Yours

JAMES DELMAGE
TARA BOERUM

DEDICATION

This book is dedicated to our children, Samantha and James—our biggest supporters, our harshest and most honest critics, and the absolute loves of our lives. For your steadfastness and refusal to lose faith in us as we've navigated this business over the past seven years, we are eternally grateful.

TABLE of CONTENTS

WELCOME to OUR KITCHEN

In 2018, I was working a job I hated, living more than a thousand miles away from my home, and feeling like the best years of my life were long gone. Then I bought a camera and everything changed.

For as long as I can remember, I've loved cooking. And it's not just any love; it's a fiery, passionate love that's full of hope, gratification, and intense satisfaction, all fueled by a desire to share it with others in my circle.

For most of my life, that circle was limited. As a kid and teenager, I cooked alongside my mom and grandma, learning and soaking up as much knowledge as I could from them, and from Lidia, Julia, and Emeril. I met Tara and cooked for her, exposing her to things she had never tried before. I cooked for my fraternity brothers, often in the wee hours of the morning after a long night at the Albany-area bars. I became a dad and cooked for my kids, and watched as their passion for food unfurled. I don't think they ever once ordered from a kids' menu!

I always felt called to the culinary world. And it was this calling, this passion, that carried me to the Best Buy in Minnetonka, Minnesota, where I purchased that little white camera and decided to start taking pictures of my food to share with others outside my circle.

My first pictures were bad. Really bad. I had to learn from scratch how to photograph food, how to use light and textures and angles and reflectors to create beautiful images. And then how to use software to edit those images into something worthy of likes and shares on Instagram, and later, clicks on YouTube.

In April 2018 I launched the Sip and Feast website with the hope of sharing my recipes with the world, but to say it was slow going at first would be an understatement. Traffic to the website was minimal and growth on Instagram was slow. I knew that the missing piece was video, but I was handcuffed by not having the space.

It was during this time that Tara and I decided to leave Minnesota and go back to New York to be closer to our family. When we first returned, we were living, temporarily, with my parents in the small apartment my grandma had lived in many years before. There was barely enough space for us to live, let alone film videos. So it wasn't until we finally bought and settled into our current home that I was able to start filming.

Much like my first photos, my first videos were bad. In fact, I invite you to watch my very first video for fried zucchini fritters to see just how bad it was. But I didn't let that—or the fact that I had two subscribers, Tara and our nephew Josh—stop me. I kept filming, each video improving slightly, as the channel grew at a snail's pace.

Then, with one video, the trajectory of Sip and Feast changed forever.

On October 8, 2021, I uploaded the video for Braised Short Rib Ragu—the image of which is the cover art for this book. It took off, and from there, the channel's subscriber count grew at a rapid pace. That, in turn, drove more and more people to the website. Things were heading in the right direction, and I was finally starting to earn money. I was struggling to do all the work on my own, though, so with a leap of faith, in April 2022 Tara left her job in financial services and joined me full time.

Together we noticed a pattern across platforms, from emails to Facebook messages to website and YouTube comments. Our readers and followers wanted something more. They wanted something tangible. They wanted a *cookbook*.

But writing a cookbook is no small undertaking, and doing it right takes time, resources, capital, and most of all, persistence and patience. Knowing that, we put the book off, but the more we put it off, the more we wanted to do it. We knew it was the missing piece of the puzzle.

And that brings us to today and the very book you now hold in your hands.

As you peruse this book, you'll notice many of the recipes are Italian American with a few non-Italian recipes sprinkled in. If you've been a reader of our website, you'll also notice that some of the recipes are our most loved and highly rated from our site, with some new and exciting ones that are exclusive to this book.

You may also notice that many of these recipes harken back to a different time. Since so many of these recipes were handed down from my grandma to my mother and me, they're deeply rooted in the past. For example, my Italian Baked Chicken and Potatoes (page 113), Fran's Pasta e Fagioli (page 163), Zucchini and Tomato Casserole (page 42), and Rigatoni with Sunday Sauce and Meatballs (page 58) are all recipes that have been passed down through generations. These recipes were not shared through written instructions, or even by word of mouth; they are dishes I learned by observing my grandma and mom, at first passively, and then more actively as I eventually took over the kitchen! In fact, many of these may have been closely guarded by our ancestors for fear that someone would steal a recipe. I have been told countless times by readers that the reason my recipes resonate with them is because they have tried for years to replicate the recipes of their dearly departed nonnas/mothers/fathers/aunts to no avail, until they came across Sip and Feast.

I'm not only honored to receive messages from readers about this, but am reinvigorated by the fact that the power of food and the nostalgia it evokes is strong; I'm so grateful it remains that way today despite all the change that takes place in the world on any given day.

My hope is that no matter which recipes you make, you use them to find some peace in a constantly changing and chaotic world, to celebrate coming together with friends and family over a meal, and maybe most importantly, to enjoy a nostalgic link to the past and to loved ones who are no longer here.

And most of all, I hope that you realize the immense gratitude Tara and I have for you, our readers, and the trust you put in us every time you make one of our recipes. It's been an honor to "show up" in your kitchen, and for that we're forever thankful.

HOW TO USE THIS BOOK

Before you begin, I want to start by saying that these recipes are not meant to be strictly adhered to. The beauty of food and recipes is that they're constantly evolving, based on the cook's location, access to ingredients, and kitchen equipment.

Italian American food looks completely different from the food in Italy because of this, and it very much deserves to be celebrated as a cuisine in its own right!

I say this because I want you to take each recipe with a proverbial grain of salt, and make tweaks as needed. If you can't find cremini mushrooms, white button mushrooms will do just fine. If you can't find scamorza cheese, use mozzarella. Don't ever feel that you're getting a lesser experience because you can't access a certain ingredient. Would I love to use truffles and Norcia sausage in my Pasta alla Norcina (page 77)? Sure! But thanks to budget and geographical constraints, I just can't, and unless you live in Umbria, it's likely you can't either.

My hope is that this book helps you feel empowered to go forth and conquer these recipes in a fearless but pragmatic way, knowing that subbing one ingredient for another will still yield beautiful results, especially when the dish is made with love!

Mise en Place

Perhaps the most important thing any home cook or professional chef can do is prepare their ingredients and tools ahead of time. This method of culinary preparation is known as *mise en place*, and it is taught in culinary school and practiced in every professional kitchen. It makes cooking so much easier, and it is something I do before every single recipe I make. I take extra time in all of my videos to address this and walk you through the mise en place for that specific recipe. Practice this a few times and you'll never go back to not doing it.

QR Codes

Many of the recipes in this cookbook have a corresponding blog post on our website, and in many instances, an accompanying YouTube video. We've included QR codes for the recipes with blog posts, so you can easily get to that recipe on our site should you want to see more details or ask a question. Simply open the camera app on your phone as if you plan to take a photo, hover over the QR code, and the link to the recipe will pop up for you to click.

Measurements

You'll notice that the ingredients in this book are shown in US volume measurements as well as in metric grams for solids and milliliters for liquids. While most of our readers are in the United States, we do have a following in Australia and Europe, and our hope is to be as inclusive with our measurements as possible.

No matter where in the world you live, for many of our dessert recipes, I do suggest using a kitchen scale and weighing the ingredients for the most accurate results. More on that in the next section.

KITCHEN ESSENTIALS

The heart of every home is a room that everyone naturally flocks to. A room that inspires, soothes, and bestows wisdom on those who gather within it. In our home, that room is the kitchen, and if you're reading this book, I'll bet it's the same for you.

If the kitchen is the heart, then the contents that fill the kitchen—the people, the ingredients, the tools—are its life force and contribute to keeping it running smoothly.

You don't need a ton of tools or ingredients for the recipes in this book, but there are a few essentials, which I'm calling out in the lists that follow. And while these lists aren't exhaustive, they do aim to provide a foundation that will help you cook with confidence. Whether you're a seasoned chef or a novice home cook, the right equipment and pantry staples can elevate your cooking from ordinary to extraordinary!

This section is all about setting you up for success, so you can focus on what matters—making amazing food for the people you love.

INGREDIENTS

Pantry Ingredients

BLACK PEPPER—I keep finely ground black pepper on hand in addition to whole black peppercorns. Depending on the recipe, the size of the grind may be different. For example, Peposo (page 175) calls for whole black peppercorns that are crushed with a mallet.

BREADCRUMBS—I usually keep plain and Italian seasoned breadcrumbs on hand.

CANNED TOMATOES—I usually keep a few different types of canned tomatoes on hand, such as whole plum tomatoes, crushed (for when I'm in a rush), passata (or tomato puree), and tomato paste.

DRIED HERBS AND SPICES—I do use some dried herbs and spices for my recipes, most notably Sicilian oregano (Italian and Greek are also great) and crushed hot red pepper flakes. Other dried spices I recommend keeping on hand are granulated garlic, garlic powder, onion powder, and bay leaves. I do *not* recommend, nor do I have in my kitchen, dried basil, or blends dubbed "Italian seasoning."

FLOUR—All-purpose is the most versatile, and it's what I've used for all the recipes in this book.

OIL

- **Extra virgin olive oil**—This is my go-to oil for most recipes in this book. It's good to have a decent extra virgin olive oil on hand for cooking, and a superior extra virgin olive oil for finishing and salads.
- **Olive oil**—Regular olive oil can come in handy for frying.
- **Neutral oil**—Avocado oil is my go-to neutral oil, but other oils, such as vegetable, canola, or sunflower oil, can also be used.

PASTA—I always keep several boxes and varieties of dried pasta on hand. Long pastas such as spaghetti, linguine, and fettuccine are great for lighter sauces, while wider pastas such as pappardelle or tagliatelle are better for heartier sauces like short rib ragu (page 86) and Bolognese (page 81), because they can hold up to the heft of the ragu. Tubular pastas such as rigatoni, ziti, and penne are also great for meat sauces, as well as baked pasta dishes. Shorter pasta shapes like ditalini, acini di pepe, orzo, and farfalline are especially great for soup.

A WORD ON PASTA WATER

Pasta should almost always be boiled in salted water. Use 2 tablespoons of fine sea or table salt per gallon of water. You'll notice that nearly every pasta recipe in this book calls for saving your pasta water. When pasta is cooked in water, it releases starch, which changes the water. Pasta water can be used to loosen a sauce that is too thick and can also emulsify sauces.

RICE—For recipes such as stuffed Cubanelles (page 141), arborio rice or any medium-grain rice can be used. If you're going to make a risotto, you may wish to consider using carnaroli rice, which is the "caviar" of risotto rice, though arborio will still get the job done.

SALT

- **Kosher salt**—Diamond Crystal kosher salt is my go-to for most recipes in this book. Any time you see a reference to *kosher salt*, I'm referring to Diamond Crystal kosher salt. I'm calling this out here because not all salt is created equal when it comes to volume measurements. For example, 1 tablespoon of table salt will contain more grains of salt than 1 tablespoon of Diamond Crystal, meaning if you swap in a different salt in the same quantity, your dish may turn out far saltier. For this reason, I suggest using Diamond Crystal salt wherever I've called for kosher salt, or adjusting the quantity as needed if you use a different brand.
- **Fine sea salt**—I use this mostly in baking recipes, but you can use fine sea salt or regular table salt to salt the water for pasta and potatoes.
- **Flaky sea salt**—A good flaky sea salt is great for finishing salads and meats!

STOCKS—For most recipes I use low-sodium stock made from either chicken or beef base; however, for best results and absolute control over sodium levels, I recommend using homemade chicken or beef stock with no added salt.

SUGAR—For most of the recipes that call for sugar, I use granulated sugar. Either white or natural is fine, and they can most often be used interchangeably. Confectioners' sugar, also known as powdered sugar, is often used for glazes and for dusting on a finished dessert.

VINEGAR—I love vinegar and the acidity it provides to so many dishes. I have a few types I always have on hand, such as white vinegar, red wine vinegar, and balsamic vinegar, but I love vinegar so much I also keep apple cider vinegar, sherry vinegar, and champagne vinegar on hand, especially for quick vinaigrettes. For many recipes, white and red wine vinegar can be used interchangeably, whereas balsamic is on the sweeter side and should really only be used when a recipe calls for it specifically.

WINE—When a recipe calls for a dry white wine, a Sauvignon Blanc or a Pinot Grigio can be used. Use what suits your budget. When a recipe calls for red wine, depending on the recipe, I may use a Chianti, Burgundy, or Cabernet. In general, these three types of red wine are good to have on hand for cooking. Again, use what suits your budget.

Miscellaneous Pantry Items

The following pantry staples are used often in our recipes, and I recommend keeping them on hand for whenever the need arises.

- **Almond paste**
- **Anchovies**
- **Baking powder**
- **Baking soda**
- **Calabrian chili paste**
- **Canned clams**
- **Cherry peppers**
- **Dijon mustard**
- **Honey**
- **Lentils**
- **Pignoli nuts (also known as pine nuts)**
- **Worcestershire sauce**

Fresh Ingredients

BUTTER—Unless otherwise noted, unsalted butter should be assumed for all my recipes. While I do keep salted butter in my house, I usually reserve that for buttering bread and don't use it when cooking or baking.

CHEESE

- **Pecorino Romano**—This salty sheep's milk cheese is my go-to for many recipes, and the one I use most often for finishing pasta dishes.
- **Parmigiano-Reggiano**—A close runner-up to pecorino, I use this cheese often for topping pastas and shaving on salads, and I use the rinds to add flavor to soups. You can substitute domestic parmesan or Grana Padano if you don't have access to Parmigiano-Reggiano.
- **Ricotta**—This creamy cheese is an essential ingredient in dishes like stuffed shells (page 90) and baked ziti (page 89). Depending on the brand you buy, some will contain more moisture than others. For example, Polly-O tends to be wetter, while Galbani is drier. Sometimes draining the ricotta is necessary for recipes like Italian cheesecake (page 213).
- **Mozzarella**—Block mozzarella is the packaged cheese you'll find in the main dairy section of your grocery store, while fresh mozzarella is often found in a separate cheese area. I use block mozzarella for dishes that require melting the cheese, such as baked ziti (page 89) and stuffed Cubanelles (page 141). Fresh mozzarella is better for use in salads and is even great on its own with a drizzle of balsamic and olive oil.

FRESH HERBS—I rely on a variety of fresh herbs for many recipes, and perhaps the most widely used one is flat-leaf Italian parsley. This is preferred over curly parsley, which tends to be used just for garnish. Other fresh herbs to keep on hand are basil, rosemary, mint, and thyme.

SUBSTITUTING DRIED HERBS FOR FRESH

The rule of thumb when substituting dried herbs for fresh is to convert at a 3:1 ratio. For every three parts fresh herbs, you'd substitute one part dried. The reason for this is that dried herbs are more potent. I do not recommend substituting dried basil for fresh, since dried has a completely different flavor and can negatively impact a recipe's results.

GARLIC—I recommend using fresh garlic cloves as opposed to pre-minced jarred garlic. I don't recommend using garlic powder or granulated garlic in place of fresh garlic, except where a recipe specifically calls for it.

LEMON—When a recipe calls for lemon juice, use *fresh squeezed* lemon juice. It makes a huge difference.

ONIONS AND SHALLOTS—I use white and yellow onions interchangeably, as their flavors are similar. I'll often use red onions for color, such as in Spinach Salad with Hot Bacon Dressing (page 199). Shallots are milder than onions and have a slight garlic flavor. I'll often use shallots when I want a gentler but still aromatic flavor, such as in vinaigrettes.

TOOLS

BAKING SHEETS—It's great to have at least a few baking sheets on hand, if space permits.

BLENDERS AND FOOD PROCESSORS—I have a standard countertop blender that I'll use for pulsing whole plum tomatoes, making drinks, and more, while I use an immersion blender for soups and vinaigrettes. I also like to have a larger capacity (14-plus-cup) food processor for easy chopping and making dough.

CANDY/DEEP-FRY THERMOMETER—This tool is really helpful to successfully fry food. It takes the guesswork out of the process.

CHEESECLOTH—This comes in particularly handy when draining ingredients, such as ricotta for Italian cheesecake (page 118).

CHEF'S KNIFE—A good sharp knife is one of the most important tools in the kitchen. My go-to is an 8-inch chef's knife.

CUTTING BOARD(S)—I keep several types of cutting boards in my kitchen. I prefer to use a wooden board, but will often use plastic boards when cutting raw meat and seafood so they can be easily cleaned either by hand or in the dishwasher. A wooden board should never be placed in the dishwasher.

DIGITAL MEAT THERMOMETERS—I recommend having both an ovenproof digital probe thermometer and an instant-read probe thermometer for accuracy and successful roasting.

DUTCH OVEN—This is highly recommended, but if you don't have one, many of the recipes that call for a Dutch oven can be made in a regular pot on the stovetop.

FRYING PANS—I use stainless steel and cast iron pans for the most part, though a nonstick pan is great for delicate fish or eggs. I recommend having a few different sizes, including 14-inch, 12-inch, and 10-inch pans.

KITCHEN SCALE—A kitchen scale is recommended, especially for baking recipes, since weighing your ingredients will yield more consistent results!

MIXERS—While a stand mixer is great because it's mainly hands-off, you can easily get away with using an electric hand mixer, especially for the recipes in this book. Where I find a stand mixer comes in handy is when kneading is required, such as with bread and pizza dough. Then I'll almost always use a stand mixer fitted with a dough hook.

PARCHMENT PAPER—A roll of parchment paper will do, but I always use the precut sheets for efficiency's sake.

PASTA SPIDER—This allows you to easily retrieve most pasta from the pot without losing any of your pasta water!

SAUCEPANS AND POTS—If space permits, it's great to have a few different-sized saucepans and pots on hand, depending on what you're making, especially a larger one for boiling pasta.

SERVING UTENSILS—A variety of different sizes and styles is always great. I'll typically reach for a large wooden spoon or ladle for short pastas, soups, and stews, and use a smaller serving spoon for things like baked artichoke hearts (page 41) or stuffed mushrooms (page 29). A serving fork comes in handy for certain meat dishes, such as prime rib (page 130).

SPATULAS—I have a few different go-to spatulas of different sizes, depending on what I'm cooking. Having a few plastic spatulas is good, as well as a thin metal fish spatula for easy turning.

SPRINGFORM PANS—These are a must for cheesecake, but also come in handy anytime you bake a cake and would like easy removal. I like to have 9-inch and 10-inch springform pans available.

TONGS—I use tongs for so many things. From serving long pastas like linguine or spaghetti to tossing salads and flipping chicken cutlets (page 118) while frying, tongs are one of my most often-used kitchen tools.

WHISKS—This tool is important for baking recipes, but also many of my savory recipes, especially when adding butter to finish a dish. It's good to have both a metal whisk and a silicone whisk for use on nonstick pans.

SMALL BITES: APPETIZERS, SNACKS, and SIDES

When it comes to small bites, I'm all about a variety of tastes and textures. It's one of the reasons I love a good antipasto platter (see page 52), charcuterie board, or tapas. There's something about grazing on a variety of different snacks that's just so exciting!

I've carefully selected our best small-bite recipes with the mindset that these can all be treated as appetizers, though many can pull double duty as sides to your favorite main courses.

When perusing this chapter, and this book in general, I invite you to keep an open mind about when to serve these dishes. If you want to make a main course out of Calamari Arrabbiata (page 37), go for it! Likewise, if you want to make an appetizer out of Tuscan-Style Balsamic-Glazed Ribs (page 138), do it! I've never been one to color within the lines when it comes to cooking, and just because I placed a recipe within a certain category doesn't mean you can't turn it into something else.

ROSEMARY TARALLI

MAKES: 32 TARALLI • **PREP:** 30 MINUTES • **COOK:** 45 MINUTES

Walk into any Italian specialty store and you're likely to find taralli: O-shaped snack crackers that come in a variety of flavors from black pepper to fennel. And while the store-bought versions are great in a pinch, nothing beats homemade taralli!

They're easy to make (the kids *love* helping me with these), are great for snacking, and make a wonderful addition to antipasto platters (see page 52) and charcuterie boards.

This particular recipe is for rosemary taralli, but you can use this recipe as a base for many other flavors! Crushed red pepper, oregano, and pecorino will yield a pizza-flavored snack, while pecorino and black pepper will create a cacio e pepe taralli. Fennel seed is also great and is the version featured on our website.

INGREDIENTS

3 cups (390 g) all-purpose flour

¾ cup (180 ml) dry white wine

½ cup (120 ml) extra virgin olive oil

2 tablespoons (12 g) dried rosemary leaves

1 tablespoon (20 g) fine sea salt, divided

INSTRUCTIONS

Combine the flour, wine, olive oil, rosemary, and 1 teaspoon of the salt in the bowl of a stand mixer and mix with the paddle attachment until combined (about 1 minute), then switch to the dough hook and mix on low speed for another 5 minutes. *Note:* If you don't have a mixer, combine the ingredients in a bowl, then transfer to a work surface and hand knead for 10 minutes.

Move the dough to a work surface and use your hands to form a loaf shape. Cover the loaf with a clean kitchen towel or plastic wrap.

Line a baking sheet with parchment paper. Pull off a small piece of the dough and roll it into a 5-inch-long rope that is roughly ½-inch thick. Connect the ends together with a slight overlap and press together. Place the tarallo onto the parchment-lined baking sheet and repeat for the remaining dough.

Bring a large pot of water to boil along with the remaining 2 teaspoons of salt. Preheat the oven to 375°F and set the rack to the middle level. Line two baking sheets with parchment paper.

Once the water comes to a boil, add 5 to 6 taralli at a time and boil just until they rise to the top of the pot (1 to 2 minutes). Remove them with a slotted spoon and place them on a paper towel–lined baking sheet to drain. After a few minutes, flip the taralli over so they dry and drain from the other side. Repeat the process until all of the taralli have been boiled.

Place the boiled and drained taralli on the parchment-lined baking sheets, about ½ inch apart. Bake for 30 to 35 minutes or until they are slightly golden, then allow to cool on the baking sheets before serving.

You shouldn't need to add any bench flour when working with taralli. In fact, you want the dough to be slightly sticky so the ends adhere to one another and don't open when boiling. If they do open, don't worry!

You can make the taralli much smaller if desired (they're normally sold this way in small bags), but the cook time will need to be reduced.

Taralli will keep for 2 weeks in a cookie tin or airtight container.

SIP & FEAST TIPS

POTATO AND HAM CROQUETTES

MAKES: 6–8 SERVINGS • **PREP:** 25 MINUTES • **COOK:** 1 HOUR, 20 MINUTES

I grew up eating potato croquettes, but it wasn't until I was an adult that I started experimenting and adding different fillings, like ham, anchovies, and various types of cheese. The first time I made potato and ham croquettes was for Tara, and we both devoured them!

I love how the crispy golden exterior gives way to the tender interior, and they're easier to make than they look. Because the flavor is relatively subtle, they're great for picky eaters, but those with more sophisticated palates love them too—after all, what's not to love about fried potatoes?

INGREDIENTS

- 2 pounds (908 g) Russet potatoes or other dry, floury potatoes
- 3 large eggs, beaten
- ½ cup (45 g) grated pecorino Romano cheese
- ¼ cup minced flat-leaf Italian parsley
- 1 teaspoon ground black pepper
- 1 teaspoon fine sea salt
- 1 tablespoon (8 g) all-purpose flour, as needed

FOR THE COATING AND FRYING

- ¼ cup (33 g) all-purpose flour, for dredging
- 3 large eggs, beaten
- 1 cup (100 g) plain breadcrumbs
- ¼ pound (113 g) ham or prosciutto, finely diced
- Neutral oil, for frying
- Fine sea salt, as needed

INSTRUCTIONS

Steam or bake the potatoes until tender, then, once they're cool enough to handle, peel and rice (see notes opposite) the potatoes.

Gently combine the riced potatoes with the eggs, cheese, parsley, pepper, and salt in a large bowl. If the mixture feels too wet to form croquettes that will hold their shape, add the flour, gently mix together, and again check the consistency. If the mixture is too dry, add a splash of water and mix again. The consistency should be wet enough to form a croquette but dry enough that it doesn't easily deform.

Using a large spoon or cookie scoop, grab roughly ¼ cup of the potato mixture and place on a parchment paper–lined baking sheet. You should have 10 to 12 scoops. Divide each potato ball in half to make 20 to 24 croquettes in all.

FOR THE COATING AND FRYING

Place the flour into a medium bowl, the eggs into a second medium bowl, and the breadcrumbs into a third medium bowl.

Grab one of the potato pieces, press it into your hands, and make an indentation. Place 1 to 2 teaspoons of the diced ham into the indentation. Fold the potato around the ham to enclose it and form an oval tubelike shape. Dip it into the flour and shake off the excess. Next, dip it into the eggs, and finally coat with the breadcrumbs. Place the breaded croquettes onto a parchment paper–lined baking sheet. At this time, they can be placed in the refrigerator to set up (see notes opposite) or fried right away.

Fill a heavy pot or high-walled saucepan with 1 inch of oil and heat to 350°F.

Once the oil reaches the frying temperature, gently place the croquettes into the oil, working in batches to avoid overcrowding the pan, and fry for 5 to 6 minutes or until golden on both sides. I recommend tasting the first croquette out of the oil (once it has cooled) to judge the salt level. If a bit more is needed, sprinkle sea salt onto the croquettes right when they come out of the oil. Serve immediately.

Use a ricing tool not only to make the process easier, but to get a fluffier consistency.

Use an oil thermometer to ensure you're frying at the proper temperature.

Placing the croquettes in the fridge for an hour to set will yield better results and prevent them from falling apart in the oil. They can also be left in the fridge to set overnight, if you like.

Potato and ham croquettes are best served promptly, but if you need to make them ahead, warm them in a 300 to 350°F oven prior to serving.

SIP & FEAST TIPS

THE EASIEST CANNELLINI DIP

MAKES: 4 SERVINGS • **PREP:** 5 MINUTES

I first made this cannellini dip on a whim. I had only a can of cannellini beans and a few other staples on hand. I was short on time but wanted to give my kids something to snack on when they got home from school. Within a few minutes I had blended the beans, lemon juice, olive oil, and garlic and was surprised by how incredibly delicious it was! I served it with some baby carrots and they enjoyed it as much as I did.

I now make this dip all the time when we're hosting a holiday or gathering because it can be *made ahead of time* (in fact, it tastes better the next day), it is budget-friendly, and is a great option for guests who are looking for something on the lighter side.

It pairs well with fresh vegetable crudités such as sliced carrots, celery, cucumber, snap peas, and cherry tomatoes, but is also great with breads such as crostini, baguette slices, or pita wedges.

INGREDIENTS

1 (15-ounce) can cannellini beans, drained

5 tablespoons (75 ml) extra virgin olive oil, plus more for serving

2 tablespoons (30 ml) fresh lemon juice

1 clove garlic

1 tablespoon rosemary leaves

1 teaspoon kosher salt, plus more to taste

¼ teaspoon cracked black pepper, plus more to taste

INSTRUCTIONS

Place all the ingredients into a food processor and pulse to combine.

Taste-test and season with salt and pepper to taste.

Scoop into a bowl, drizzle with olive oil, and serve.

Be sure to drain the beans very well to avoid a runny dip.

If the dip is too dry for your liking, add a teaspoon of water at a time to loosen it up.

Fresh rosemary sprigs make a beautiful garnish!

SIP & FEAST TIPS

EGGPLANT CAPONATA

MAKES: 6 SERVINGS • **PREP:** 10 MINUTES • **COOK:** 1 HOUR

This incredible sweet-and-sour Sicilian-style appetizer combines eggplant, peppers, onions, olives, capers, pignoli nuts, and raisins. I love it slathered on some crusty bread, as a sandwich topping, or by itself. Adding it to pasta is also a great option.

The thing I like best about *homemade* caponata is that it is far more economical than store-bought. Caponata is often sold in relatively small jars in Italian specialty stores, and while it's good in a pinch, homemade is vastly superior in every way!

FOR THE ROASTED EGGPLANT

- 2 pounds (908 g) eggplant, cut into 1½-inch cubes
- ½ cup (120 ml) extra virgin olive oil, plus more if needed
- 1 teaspoon kosher salt
- ½ teaspoon black ground pepper

FOR THE CAPONATA

- ⅓ cup (45 g) pignoli nuts
- ¼ cup (60 ml) extra virgin olive oil
- 3 celery ribs, chopped
- 1 large red bell pepper, chopped
- 1 medium red onion, sliced
- 1 (6-ounce) can tomato paste
- ¼ teaspoon crushed hot red pepper flakes
- 1 cup (140 g) chopped pitted green olives
- ¼ cup (42 g) packed black raisins, optional
- 2 tablespoons (18 g) capers, rinsed
- 2 tablespoons (26 g) granulated sugar
- ¼ cup (60 ml) red wine vinegar
- Salt and pepper, to taste
- ¼ cup minced flat-leaf Italian parsley
- 3 tablespoons mint and/or basil leaves, for garnish

FOR THE ROASTED EGGPLANT

Preheat the oven to 425°F and set the rack to the middle level. Toss the cubed eggplant with the olive oil, salt, and pepper, then spread the eggplant onto parchment paper–lined baking sheet(s), making sure to not overcrowd the pieces. Roast for 30 to 40 minutes or until fully cooked through and soft in the middle.

FOR THE CAPONATA

Toast the pignoli nuts in a dry medium pan over medium-low heat for approximately 5 minutes, watching carefully to prevent burning. Once toasted, set them aside.

Heat the olive oil in a large frying pan over medium heat. Add the celery, bell pepper, and onion and sauté for 5 to 7 minutes or until softened, then add the tomato paste and continue to cook for another 5 minutes, stirring frequently. If the paste starts to burn, add a little water to the pan. Then add the red pepper flakes and cook for 30 seconds.

Add the olives, raisins, capers, sugar, and red wine vinegar and cook for 5 minutes, allowing the vinegar and sugar to cook through and incorporate. Then add the roasted eggplant to the pan and gently mix it all, taking care not to crush the eggplant. Taste-test to assess the acidity and add more sugar or vinegar if required. Season with salt and black pepper to taste.

When satisfied with the taste, turn off the heat and add the parsley and toasted pignoli nuts. Mix well and serve garnished with mint or basil.

Caponata can be eaten right away, but it's better to refrigerate overnight so that the flavors meld together.

Olives and capers are inherently salty, which is why the salt in this recipe was kept to a minimum. Be sure to salt to taste after *you've added them.*

Raisins can be omitted, but if doing so you will most likely need more sugar to balance out the vinegar.

STUFFED MUSHROOMS

MAKES: 6 SERVINGS • **PREP:** 20 MINUTES • **COOK:** 35 MINUTES

I've been making these Italian-style stuffed mushrooms for decades now and they continue to be one of my favorites! Not only are they loved by my family, but since I published the recipe to my blog five years ago I've received countless comments, messages, and emails about them!

These are addicting; it's impossible to eat just one. If you plan to make these for a gathering, you may want to double the recipe. And if you're just making them for yourself, you might also want to double the recipe!

They're easy and fun to make with the kids; Sammy and James always loved to help with removing the stems and scooping the stuffing into the mushroom caps.

INGREDIENTS

- 1½ pounds (680 g) white or baby bella mushrooms (see notes below)
- ½ cup (120 ml) extra virgin olive oil
- 6 cloves garlic, minced
- ¼ teaspoon crushed hot red pepper flakes
- ½ cup (120 ml) dry white wine
- 2 cups (480 ml) low-sodium chicken stock, divided
- 3 tablespoons (45 ml) fresh lemon juice
- 1 cup (100 g) plain breadcrumbs
- ½ cup plus 2 tablespoons (56 g) grated Parmigiano-Reggiano cheese, divided
- ½ cup minced flat-leaf Italian parsley
- 1½ teaspoons kosher salt, plus more as needed
- Freshly ground black pepper, to taste
- 1 large lemon, cut into wedges, for serving

INSTRUCTIONS

Preheat the oven to 425°F and set the rack to the second-highest level. Cut off the very ends (woody part) of the mushroom stems and discard. Remove the good part of the stems and mince. Set aside ¾ cup of the minced stems and save the remaining stems for another purpose or discard.

Heat the olive oil in a large frying pan over medium-low heat and add the garlic. Sauté the garlic until golden, then add the red pepper flakes and cook for 30 seconds. Next, turn the heat to medium, add the minced mushroom stems, and cook for 5 minutes, stirring occasionally.

Add the wine and cook for 2 minutes to reduce slightly, then add ½ cup of the chicken stock, the lemon juice, breadcrumbs, ½ cup of the cheese, the parsley, and salt. Mix well, turn off the heat, and taste-test. Adjust the salt and pepper if required. If the stuffing is too dry, add a bit more stock (it should be very moist).

Use a spoon to scoop the stuffing into the mushroom caps, and save any remaining stuffing. Place the stuffed mushrooms into a large baking dish and pour in the remaining 1½ cups of chicken stock. Sprinkle no more than ¼ cup of the remaining stuffing mixture into the stock and sprinkle the remaining 2 tablespoons of Parmigiano-Reggiano on top of the mushrooms.

Bake for 20 to 25 minutes or until tender. If needed, broil for the last 60 seconds to brown the top. Spoon the residual liquid from the bottom of the baking dish on top of the mushrooms and serve with lemon wedges.

Large stuffing mushrooms, small white button mushrooms, or baby bella mushrooms all work well for this recipe.

To clean your mushrooms, use a slightly damp paper towel to gently remove the dirt. Don't wash or submerge them in water.

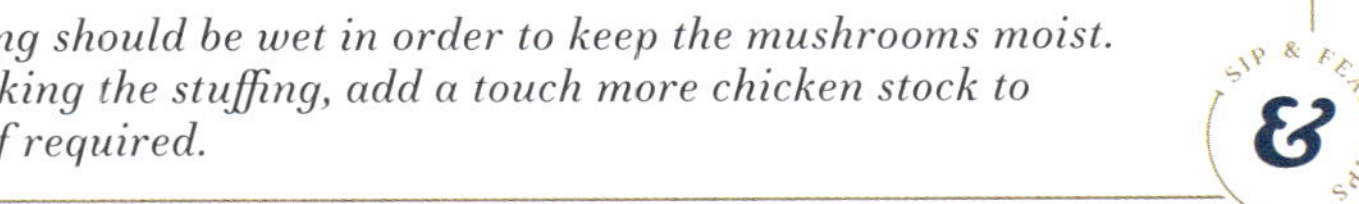

The stuffing should be wet in order to keep the mushrooms moist. When making the stuffing, add a touch more chicken stock to moisten, if required.

SIP & FEAST TIPS

ROASTED RED PEPPERS

MAKES: 8 SERVINGS • **PREP:** 10 MINUTES • **COOK:** 60 MINUTES

I grew up eating store-bought roasted red peppers, mainly on holidays as part of an antipasto platter, and they were always just okay. As an adult, I found that the jars were just way too expensive, so one day I made my own homemade roasted red peppers, and I've never looked back. Not only is the homemade version more economical, especially if you grow your own peppers, but the taste of store-bought just doesn't compare!

Roasted red peppers make a great addition to sandwiches, Italian chopped salads, or antipasto spreads, and can even be used to make sauce for pasta. My personal favorite way to enjoy them is on a baguette with fresh mozzarella, sliced prosciutto, arugula, and balsamic glaze. So good!

INGREDIENTS

6 large red bell peppers

½ cup (120 ml) extra virgin olive oil, plus more if needed

2 cloves garlic, sliced, optional

3 tablespoons minced flat-leaf Italian parsley

1 teaspoon kosher salt

INSTRUCTIONS

Preheat the oven to 450°F. Place the bell peppers on a baking sheet and roast for 20 minutes, then flip them over and roast for another 20 to 25 minutes or until the peppers are well charred on all sides. Quickly place the peppers into a bowl and cover with plastic wrap for 15 to 20 minutes to steam.

Once the peppers are cool enough to handle, use your hands to peel and remove their skins, then cut them in half and remove the stems and seeds. The peppers can be left as large halves or sliced into smaller pieces or strips.

Transfer the peppers to a bowl and add the olive oil, garlic, if using, parsley, and salt. Let the peppers sit for at least 1 hour before eating or refrigerate overnight.

Do not rinse the peppers to remove the seeds or skin, since that will remove a lot of the roasted flavor.

If you own a gas stove, you can char the peppers with long tongs over the flame to save time rather than roasting in the oven. Additionally, a grill works great for charring the peppers.

Adding garlic is optional, but highly encouraged!

The peppers can be stored in the refrigerator for up to 5 days.

SIP & FEAST TIPS

SPIEDINI ALLA ROMANA

MAKES: 4–6 SERVINGS • **PREP:** 20 MINUTES • **COOK:** 20 MINUTES

If you've never tried spiedini alla Romana, you are in for a real treat! The combination of the toasted bread and fresh mozzarella is indulgent, and the buttery caper-anchovy sauce is arguably drinkable.

Often in restaurants you'll find spiedini skewered with a steak knife. We're using metal skewers, as they give a beautiful presentation, but you can also use wooden skewers or choose to remove the skewers prior to serving.

This appetizer is truly impressive, making it perfect for gatherings and dinner parties (see page 158).

FOR THE SAUCE

3 tablespoons (45 ml) extra virgin olive oil

1 medium shallot, minced

6 large anchovy fillets

5 cloves garlic, sliced

1½ cups (360 ml) low-sodium chicken stock

½ cup (120 ml) dry white wine

¼ cup minced flat-leaf Italian parsley

3 tablespoons (27 g) capers, drained and rinsed

1 tablespoon (15 ml) fresh lemon juice

6 tablespoons (84 g) butter, cubed

Freshly ground black pepper, to taste

FOR THE SPIEDINI

1 pound (454 g) fresh mozzarella cheese, sliced

1 large loaf Italian bread (about 1 pound/454 g), cut into ½-inch-thick slices

2 cloves garlic

Nonstick cooking spray

INSTRUCTIONS

Preheat the oven to 500°F.

FOR THE SAUCE

Heat the olive oil and shallot in a large saucepan over medium heat. After 1 minute, add the anchovies and garlic and cook until golden. Smash the anchovies with a wooden spoon to help them dissolve. Add the stock and wine and bring the mixture to a boil. Add the parsley, capers, and lemon juice and reduce the heat to a simmer.

Whisk in the butter, 1 cube at a time, until a smooth sauce forms. Add some pepper to the sauce and taste for salt. You will probably not need to add any salt due to the inherent saltiness of the capers and anchovies. Turn the heat to the lowest level to keep the sauce warm.

FOR THE SPIEDINI

Blot the mozzarella with a paper towel to remove any excess moisture. Lay the bread pieces out on a baking sheet and toast them for 2 to 3 minutes. Once the bread comes out, rub each piece with a garlic clove.

Top each piece of bread with a slice of mozzarella and another piece of bread. Repeat until you have 3 to 4 stacked sandwiches. Turn them onto their sides and place 1 to 2 large skewers into each section to hold them together. Place the skewered sandwiches on a foil-lined baking sheet that has been sprayed with nonstick cooking spray.

Bake for 10 to 12 minutes or until browned on all sides. To achieve even cooking, turn the skewers every few minutes. Also, once the cheese starts to melt, be sure to press each skewer section together so that the cheese sticks to the bread on both sides.

Place the spiedini onto a platter and pour the sauce over the top and onto the platter. Serve immediately.

You can use many types of bread for this dish. Rustic loaves or country white bread cut into squares would be great options.

Traditionally, spiedini alla Romana is made with fresh mozzarella. We suggest using that over block mozzarella. For a shortcut, look for presliced fresh mozzarella at the grocery store.

Be sure to rinse the capers well, as they are quite salty. The rinse helps to remove some of the salt.

SIP & FEAST TIPS &

BAKED CLAMS

MAKES: 4 SERVINGS • **PREP:** 10 MINUTES • **COOK:** 10 MINUTES

Where I grew up on Long Island, baked clams, or clams oreganata, are almost as ubiquitous as bagels and pizza! They can be found on the menu of nearly every Italian American restaurant, and in every seafood joint and clam shack. They also happen to be a favorite appetizer for Christmas Eve, when many Italian American families feature them as one of the traditional seven "fishes."

The garlicky breadcrumbs and fresh lemon are the perfect match for the briny clams. The dish may look complicated, but it really is quite easy to make.

My favorite way to enjoy baked clams is alongside other homemade seafood favorites, like fried calamari and shrimp scampi rolls, along with an ice-cold beer!

INGREDIENTS

- 2 dozen littleneck clams, scrubbed (see notes below)
- ½ cup (50 g) plain breadcrumbs
- 2 cloves garlic, minced
- 3 tablespoons minced flat-leaf Italian parsley
- ½ teaspoon kosher salt
- ½ teaspoon dried oregano
- ¼ teaspoon crushed hot red pepper flakes
- ¾ cup (180 ml) clam juice or chicken stock, divided
- ¼ cup (60 ml) extra virgin olive oil, divided
- 1 tablespoon (15 ml) fresh lemon juice
- ¼ cup (60 ml) dry white wine
- 2 tablespoons (28 g) butter
- 1 large lemon, cut into wedges, for serving

INSTRUCTIONS

Preheat the oven to 425°F. Place the clams on a baking sheet and bake in the oven for a few minutes until they open slightly, then carefully open each clam by sliding a butter knife all the way toward the joint and then rotating. Discard the top shell and any clams that do not open. Gently dislodge the clam from its shell, then place it back in the shell. Set the oven rack to the second-highest level and turn on the broiler to high.

In a large bowl combine the breadcrumbs, garlic, parsley, salt, oregano, red pepper flakes, ¼ cup of the clam juice, 2 tablespoons of the olive oil, and the lemon juice. Mix well, taste, and adjust the salt and red pepper flakes as needed. If the breadcrumbs aren't moist enough to hold together when pressed, add a bit more of the clam juice.

Use a spoon to pack the breadcrumb mixture over the clams in their shells. This will seal the clams in tight so they stay moist during cooking.

Place the stuffed clams in a baking pan and add the remaining ½ cup of clam juice, the wine, and butter to the pan. Sprinkle a bit of the remaining breadcrumbs (no more than 2 tablespoons worth) into the clam juice. Drizzle the remaining 2 tablespoons of olive oil onto each clam and place the pan under the broiler for 5 to 7 minutes. Watch carefully to prevent burning.

When the stuffed clams are golden brown, transfer them to a serving dish and pour the pan juices into the dish around the clams so anyone can spoon on extra juice if they like. Serve with the lemon wedges.

Clams are filter feeders and tend to hold onto a lot of sand that needs to be removed before they're cooked. Most commercial clams will already have been purged by the time you buy them, but you'll occasionally need to purge them yourself. Your best bet is to ask your fishmonger if they've been purged.

Open the clams over a large baking sheet to capture all of their juice. This extra clam juice can be strained and used in the recipe, or you can use store-bought clam juice.

The breadcrumb mixture should be moist so the clams don't dry out during the broiling process. If they're at all dry, be sure to drizzle with enough extra virgin olive oil to thoroughly moisten them before broiling.

SIP & FEAST TIPS

Frozen squid is often fresher than the squid sitting at the seafood counter. I recommend buying frozen; simply thaw before using.

Calamari arrabbiata is better when eaten promptly! Call everyone to the table before it's ready; otherwise the sauce can make the calamari soggy. Keep in mind though that no matter how fast it's eaten, the calamari won't be as crisp as traditional fried calamari.

Feel free to slice up some cherry peppers, flour them, and fry them up too. Fried cherry pepper slices are heavenly!

CALAMARI ARRABBIATA

MAKES: 4 SERVINGS • **PREP:** 20 MINUTES • **MARINATE:** 30 MINUTES • **COOK:** 20 MINUTES

I first had calamari arrabbiata at one of my favorite family-style restaurants on Long Island, La Parma in Huntington. The calamari was lightly battered and fried, then tossed with a heavenly cherry pepper, garlic, and tomato sauce. It was truly one of the most flavorful dishes I had ever had, and I knew I needed to replicate it in my own kitchen.

This dish is great for those who enjoy a little extra heat. It's a wonderful choice for Christmas Eve's Feast of the Seven Fishes, but equally good for a quiet night at home!

FOR THE SAUCE

¼ cup (60 g) extra virgin olive oil

15 cloves garlic, roughly chopped

1 (6-ounce) can tomato paste

¾ cup (115 g) quartered jarred cherry peppers (stems and seeds removed), divided

1 (28-ounce) can plum tomatoes, hand crushed or pulsed in a blender

Salt and pepper, to taste

¼ cup packed basil leaves, hand torn

FOR THE CALAMARI

1 pound (454 g) squid, cleaned, tubes cut into ½-inch circles and tentacles left whole

1 cup (240 ml) milk

1 teaspoon kosher salt

Neutral oil, for frying

1 cup (130 g) all-purpose flour

½ cup (65 g) cornstarch

½ teaspoon baking powder

¾ teaspoon ground black pepper

FOR THE SAUCE

Heat the olive oil and garlic in a large saucepan over medium heat. Once the garlic is golden, add the tomato paste and cook for 5 minutes, stirring frequently. Add a touch of water and/or lower the heat if the paste starts to burn. Add ½ cup of the cherry peppers and cook for 1 minute.

Add the plum tomatoes and bring the sauce to a lively simmer for about 5 minutes. The sauce should be quite thick. Make sure to taste-test and season with salt and black pepper if required. Keep the sauce on low heat to keep warm.

FOR THE CALAMARI

Meanwhile, preheat the oven to 200°F. Place the squid, milk, and salt into a large bowl and stir to combine. Refrigerate for at least 30 minutes.

While the calamari soaks, heat at least 3 inches of neutral oil to 360 to 370°F in a deep cast iron or heavy pot.

Line a baking sheet with parchment paper and set aside. In a large bowl, whisk the flour, cornstarch, baking powder, and pepper together.

Drain the calamari and pat it dry. Working in batches, add the calamari to the flour mixture and toss to coat. Place the coated calamari pieces onto the parchment paper–lined baking sheet. Repeat the process for the remaining pieces.

Again working in batches, gently place the floured calamari into the hot oil and fry for 2 to 4 minutes or until golden. Do not crowd the pan.

Remove the calamari with a slotted spoon and place onto a wire rack. Place it into the oven to keep warm while working on subsequent batches. Remove any bits of flour from the oil and fry the next batch. Repeat the process until all the calamari is fried.

Pour 1¼ cups of the sauce into a large bowl. Add the calamari and basil leaves and toss to coat, adding a touch more sauce if needed (you don't want to flood the calamari with sauce). Place the calamari arrabbiata on a platter and top with the remaining ¼ cup cherry peppers. Serve with the remaining sauce on the side. Enjoy!

ITALIAN SEAFOOD SALAD

MAKES: 6 SERVINGS • **PREP:** 25 MINUTES • **BRINE TIME:** 15 MINUTES • **COOK:** 2 MINUTES

When it comes to hosting and entertaining, I'm always looking for dishes that can be made ahead and have outrageous flavor. This seafood salad checks both boxes in a major way. This dish gets even better after spending some time in the fridge, and the fact that it can be made a day in advance frees up more time for prepping other dishes that are better served fresh, and for any last-minute cleaning. (Who are we kidding—the cleaning is always done last minute!)

I love the juxtaposition of textures and flavors here too—the tender calamari and plump shrimp with the crunchy celery is a delight for the senses. The olives give a nice salty bite, and the smoky roasted red peppers are complemented by the brightness of the lemon.

This is another one that's just perfect for Christmas Eve's Feast of the Seven Fishes, but so good and simple you can really make it for any occasion or gathering!

FOR THE SEAFOOD

¾ pound (340 g) squid, cleaned, tubes cut into ½-inch circles and any large tentacles cut in half

¾ pound (340 g) large shrimp, deveined and shells and tails removed (31–40 count work well)

1 teaspoon kosher salt

½ teaspoon baking soda

FOR THE SALAD

1 cup (100 g) chopped celery

½ cup (70 g) chopped roasted red peppers

½ cup (70 g) Sicilian green olives, pitted and sliced

¼ cup (40 g) diced red onion

¼ cup minced flat-leaf Italian parsley

1 clove garlic, grated

¼ teaspoon crushed hot red pepper flakes, plus more to taste

½ cup (120 ml) extra virgin olive oil, plus more to taste

¼ cup (60 ml) fresh lemon juice, plus more to taste

Salt, to taste

FOR THE SEAFOOD

In a large bowl, combine the squid and shrimp with the salt, baking soda, and enough water to cover and set aside for 15 minutes.

FOR THE SALAD

Place the celery, red peppers, olives, onion, parsley, garlic, red pepper flakes, olive oil, and lemon juice into a large bowl and mix together.

Set up a bowl of ice water and bring a large pot of water to boil.

Drain the squid and shrimp well, then boil for 2 minutes or until cooked through. Using a slotted spoon, place the cooked seafood in the ice water bath immediately.

Once the seafood is cold, drain and add to the salad and mix together. Taste-test and season with salt to taste.

Chill the seafood salad in the fridge for at least a couple of hours. Before serving, taste-test again and add more olive oil, lemon juice, or salt and red pepper flakes if required. Enjoy!

I recommend using squid that are roughly 6 inches long. If using very large squid, it's best to cut thinner rings and cut the tentacles in half or quarters.

Any size shrimp will work, but large shrimp (31–40 count) will cook at the same rate as the squid. If using larger shrimp, add them to the boiling water 1 to 2 minutes before the squid or cook them separately.

It's best to chill the salad for a few hours, but even better overnight!

STAUB

BAKED ARTICHOKE HEARTS

MAKES: 4 SERVINGS • **PREP:** 10 MINUTES • **COOK:** 20 MINUTES

Baked artichoke hearts with seasoned breadcrumbs is the easy dish I make when I'm craving stuffed artichokes but don't have the time to make them. With most of the same ingredients as stuffed artichokes, these artichoke hearts are packed with so much flavor and are easily one of our readers' favorite recipes!

This dish is especially popular around Thanksgiving but is great any time of year. I've served this as an appetizer, but it's also great as a side dish alongside almost any main course!

INGREDIENTS

½ cup (50 g) plain breadcrumbs

½ cup (45 g) grated Parmigiano-Reggiano cheese

¼ cup minced flat-leaf Italian parsley

¼ cup (60 ml) dry white wine

1 tablespoon (15 ml) fresh lemon juice

½ teaspoon kosher salt

¼ cup (60 ml) extra virgin olive oil

3 cloves garlic, minced

3 (14-ounce) cans artichoke hearts, drained and rinsed

¼ teaspoon crushed hot red pepper flakes

INSTRUCTIONS

Preheat the oven to 375°F and set the rack to the middle level. In a large bowl, mix together the breadcrumbs, cheese, parsley, wine, lemon juice, and salt and set aside.

In a small bowl, mix the olive oil and garlic together. Spoon half of the garlic oil into a large baking dish and spread it around to evenly distribute. Place the artichoke hearts into the baking dish and top them with the remaining garlic oil and the red pepper flakes.

Evenly sprinkle the seasoned breadcrumbs onto the artichoke hearts and bake for 15 to 20 minutes or until the breadcrumbs have browned. For more color, the artichoke hearts can be broiled for the last 45 to 60 seconds, but watch carefully to prevent burning.

I prefer to use canned artichoke hearts for this recipe, but you can use frozen. Just be sure to defrost and drain them prior to using. I do not recommend using marinated artichoke hearts, as doing so may alter the flavor of the dish.

Feel free to add other ingredients, such as mint, lemon zest, or toasted pignoli nuts. These would all nicely complement the dish!

SIP & FEAST TIPS

ZUCCHINI AND TOMATO CASSEROLE

MAKES: 6 SERVINGS • **PREP:** 20 MINUTES • **COOK:** 45 MINUTES

When it comes to matrilineal traditions, this casserole is near the top of my list. I can remember my grandmother making this with zucchini from our garden, my mom still makes it to this day, and now I make it for my family. I hope my kids continue the tradition and make it for their future children.

I love how the layers of tomato, zucchini, and onion marry with the pecorino, breadcrumbs, and oregano, and to say our house smells fantastic as this cooks is an understatement!

While this casserole is wonderful in summer when there is almost an overabundance of zucchini, I do make it all year round and almost always on Thanksgiving. It makes a great side dish to many main courses, and the leftovers are phenomenal reheated on the stovetop with a few over-easy eggs lightly fried in olive oil and topped with Calabrian chili paste.

FOR THE SEASONED BREADCRUMBS

½ cup (50 g) plain breadcrumbs

¼ cup (23 g) finely grated pecorino Romano cheese

2 cloves garlic, minced

1 teaspoon dried Sicilian oregano

½ teaspoon crushed hot red pepper flakes

3 tablespoons (45 ml) extra virgin olive oil

FOR THE CASSEROLE

3 medium zucchini

2 large slicing tomatoes

2 large yellow onions

½ cup (120 ml) extra virgin olive oil, divided

¼ cup (23 g) finely grated pecorino Romano cheese, plus more for topping

2 teaspoons dried Sicilian oregano

Salt and pepper, to taste

INSTRUCTIONS

Preheat the oven to 375°F and set the rack to the middle level.

FOR THE SEASONED BREADCRUMBS

In a medium bowl, mix together all the ingredients for the seasoned breadcrumbs and set aside.

FOR THE CASSEROLE

Use a mandoline or sharp knife to thinly slice the zucchini lengthwise and to thinly slice the tomatoes and onions. Drain the sliced tomatoes and pat dry the tomatoes and zucchini with paper towels before moving on to the next step.

Oil a 9-x-13-inch baking dish with about 1 tablespoon of the olive oil and place a few layers of zucchini on the bottom. Drizzle with the olive oil, sprinkle on some of the cheese, and season with some oregano and salt and pepper. Next, add a few layers of onions, drizzle with the olive oil, and sprinkle with the cheese and seasonings in the same manner. Finally, layer the tomatoes over the top, drizzle with the olive oil, sprinkle with the cheese, and season. Sprinkle the breadcrumbs on top and grate a bit more cheese over the breadcrumbs. Drizzle with more oil if required. The breadcrumbs should be well moistened.

Bake for 45 minutes or until bubbly. Most of the liquid should be evaporated at this point. If the breadcrumbs aren't golden brown, you can broil for the last 1 to 2 minutes, but watch very carefully. Wait at least 10 to 15 minutes before serving so that the juices settle.

Whenever you're using a mandoline, it's important to follow the manufacturer's instructions for safety. Always use the safety guard and take your time. You can also use a sharp knife instead.

A large, shallow baking dish with only three layers works better and cooks quicker than a deep dish with many layers of ingredients, but both will work.

Distribute a portion of the seasoning on each layer. Depending on how many layers are made, a bit more or less seasoning might be required.

Cooking times are a rough estimate. Bake until most of the liquid evaporates and the zucchini is clear and tender. If the casserole is wet after 45 minutes of baking you can carefully drain some of the liquid or pull it out with a bulb baster or paper towels, then bake for another 5 to 10 minutes before serving.

WHITE BEANS WITH KALE, TOMATOES, AND GARLIC

MAKES: 4 SERVINGS • **PREP:** 5 MINUTES • **COOK:** 30 MINUTES

Tara has been making this dish for years now, and each time she makes it she changes it up a bit. Sometimes she adds breadcrumbs, and other times she'll add crumbled sausage or even sliced sun-dried tomatoes. At its core, it's a simple combination of cannellini beans, roasted cherry tomatoes, and kale with a lot of garlic! We keep the garlic cloves whole here and cook them in the olive oil until golden and tender, which gives the garlic a buttery texture and mellow flavor.

While we often eat this as a side dish, it can be an appetizer, or even a main course. It's also great tossed with rigatoni or penne. Feel free to add a good drizzle of extra virgin olive oil and a sprinkle of grated Parmigiano-Reggiano cheese at the end, if desired.

INGREDIENTS

12 ounces (340 g) cherry tomatoes

½ cup (120 ml) extra virgin olive oil, divided, plus more for serving

¼ teaspoon kosher salt, plus more to taste

10 cloves garlic

1 pound (454 g) curly green kale, hand torn, ribs and large stems removed

1 (15-ounce) can cannellini beans, drained but not rinsed

¼ teaspoon crushed hot red pepper flakes

INSTRUCTIONS

Preheat the oven to 450°F. Toss the cherry tomatoes with 2 tablespoons of the olive oil and the salt. Spread the tomatoes on a parchment paper–lined baking sheet and roast them for 15 to 20 minutes or until wilted and charred.

While the tomatoes roast, heat a large frying pan over medium-low heat. Once hot, add the remaining 6 tablespoons of extra virgin olive oil and the garlic cloves. Sauté the cloves until they are golden on all sides, then remove them with a slotted spoon and set aside.

Add the kale to the pan and mix well to coat with the oil. Turn the heat to medium, cover with a tight-fitting lid, and cook for 5 minutes, then remove the lid. If there is too much liquid in the pan, turn the heat to medium-high and cook for 1 to 2 minutes more, or until the liquid has evaporated.

Taste the kale to check for doneness, then add the beans and red pepper flakes and cook for another 3 minutes to warm them through. Taste-test and adjust the salt as needed. Once satisfied, turn off the heat and toss with the roasted cherry tomatoes and cooked garlic. Drizzle with extra virgin olive oil and serve.

Canned beans often have added sodium. For this reason, do not adjust the salt level until after you've added the cannellini beans and taste-tested.

Purple kale or Tuscan kale can also be used.

Anchovies add tremendous flavor to this dish! If you plan to use them, add 1 to 2 fillets at the same time as the garlic.

BRUSSELS SPROUTS WITH BACON, WALNUTS, AND GOAT CHEESE

MAKES: 6 SERVINGS • **PREP:** 15 MINUTES • **COOK:** 35 MINUTES

This incredible dish packs a ton of flavor and is one of our newest favorites. Tara and I recently visited the restaurant and inn where my brother works, the Watershed in Jamesport, New York, and a similar dish was on their appetizer menu. We ordered it and loved it so much that we decided to put our own twist on it and add it to the cookbook.

This makes a fantastic appetizer, but can absolutely be served as a side dish, especially for Thanksgiving!

INGREDIENTS

- 3 pounds (1.4 kg) brussels sprouts, ends trimmed, outer leaves removed, and halved
- ⅓ cup (80 ml) extra virgin olive oil
- 1½ teaspoons kosher salt
- ¼ teaspoon ground black pepper
- ½ pound (226 g) bacon, cut into ¼-inch pieces
- 1 cup (140 g) coarsely chopped walnuts
- 1 tablespoon (15 ml) honey, plus more for drizzling
- 4 ounces (113 g) goat cheese, crumbled
- 1 tablespoon thyme leaves

INSTRUCTIONS

Preheat the oven to 450°F and set the rack to the middle level.

In a large bowl, toss the brussels sprouts with the olive oil, salt, and pepper. Place on a parchment paper–lined baking sheet, cut side down, and roast for 20 to 25 minutes or until well charred.

While the sprouts roast, heat a medium nonstick pan over medium-low heat and add the bacon. Cook it until it's crispy and most of the fat has rendered, 7 to 10 minutes, then use a slotted spoon to remove the bacon and drain on a paper towel–lined dish. Leave roughly ¼ cup (60 grams) of bacon fat in the pan.

Add the walnuts to the pan and cook in the bacon fat for 1 to 2 minutes to warm through, then turn off the heat, add half of the bacon back to the pan, and set aside.

Once the sprouts are roasted, remove them from the oven and place in a serving bowl. Toss them with the bacon-walnut mixture and the honey and allow to cool for 5 to 10 minutes.

Add the goat cheese crumbles and thyme and toss gently, then taste-test and adjust the salt and pepper if needed. Top with the remaining bacon and a drizzle of honey if desired, and serve immediately.

SIP & FEAST TIPS

Bacon is much easier to slice into lardons when it's frozen! I usually keep 6-to-8-ounce portions of bacon in my freezer to use in a pinch.

Many grocery stores sell already crumbled goat cheese. I find that the quality of the cheese isn't nearly as good as block goat cheese, so opt for that if possible. Keep in mind that goat cheese will be much easier to crumble if it's cold!

Pecans or hazelnuts would also be great in place of the walnuts.

ROASTED ASPARAGUS WITH LEMON AND PARMESAN

MAKES: 6 SERVINGS • **PREP:** 5 MINUTES • **COOK:** 18 MINUTES

One of the reasons I love asparagus is that it really doesn't need much manipulation; from prep, to cook time, to seasoning, it's one of the simplest vegetables to work with. The ends can be removed with only your hands, it needs very little time in the oven, and it's quite good with just olive oil, salt, and pepper. But, as with many other dishes, a bit of lemon and cheese elevates your basic roasted asparagus in a huge way.

I make this dish all the time because it's just that easy, and while I serve it as a side dish, it can definitely pull double duty as an appetizer. It can even be served at room temperature, or chilled—the choice is yours!

INGREDIENTS

2 bunches asparagus, woody ends removed

¼ cup (60 ml) extra virgin olive oil

Salt and pepper, to taste

1 lemon, zested

Grated Parmigiano-Reggiano cheese, to taste

INSTRUCTIONS

Preheat the oven to 425°F and set the rack to the middle level.

Lay the asparagus on a parchment-lined baking sheet, coat it with the olive oil, and add salt and pepper to taste.

Roast the asparagus in the oven for 12 to 18 minutes or until tender.

Sprinkle the roasted asparagus with the lemon zest and cheese and serve.

Use as much or as little Parmigiano-Reggiano as you'd like. Likewise, you can increase or decrease the amount of lemon zest depending on your personal preference.

Thinner asparagus tends to be more tender and will take less time to cook, while thicker asparagus will take longer. Test the asparagus with a fork to determine when it's done to your liking.

TOMATO CONFIT

MAKES: 12 SERVINGS • **PREP:** 20 MINUTES • **COOK:** 40 MINUTES

Tomato confit with garlic is a simple condiment that's packed with flavor and so easy to make. It's excellent served warm with lots of crusty bread for dipping, but it can also be used to top bruschetta, grilled chicken, fish, salads, sandwiches, and more.

We recommend using cherry or grape tomatoes for this recipe since they are thin-skinned and have less moisture. Other tomatoes, such as beefsteak or heirloom, have too much water and may not yield the best results. Use any color cherry tomatoes you'd like!

INGREDIENTS

- 24 ounces (680 g) cherry or grape tomatoes
- 1 cup (136 g) garlic cloves (3 to 4 heads worth)
- 10 sprigs thyme
- ¼ teaspoon crushed hot red pepper flakes, or 2 dried whole chili peppers
- 1¾ cups (420 ml) extra virgin olive oil

INSTRUCTIONS

Place all the ingredients in a large saucepan or pot and cook over low heat until the garlic turns golden and soft, but not burned. After 35 to 40 minutes, the garlic should be golden and very soft and most of the tomatoes will have burst. Turn off the heat and let the contents cool for 1 hour.

Serve with crusty bread or use it as a topping for chicken or fish. For storage, pour into a pint-sized mason jar and refrigerate (see notes below).

Eat right away while it's warm and spread onto crusty bread. It's also delicious atop fish or chicken.

Never store garlic or tomato confit outside of the fridge. Garlic is a low-acid ingredient, and when stored with oil in a warm environment it can produce the toxins that cause botulism. Once the confit cools, store it in an airtight jar, taking care that the garlic is completely covered by oil. We recommend eating within 3 days.

SIP & FEAST TIPS &

BUILDING AN EPIC ANTIPASTO PLATTER

The Italian antipasto platter is a wondrous thing! There's nothing better than watching a guest's eyes light up when they see a beautiful antipasto board. And it's equally wonderful for the host—since it's made ahead of time, it allows whoever is hosting to relax and engage with their guests.

With an array of items to choose from, including pickled veggies, crackers, salty cured meats, olives, and more, there's something here for everyone! You do not need to be a food stylist to create a beautiful antipasto board. There are a few tips and tricks I've picked up along the way, and I'm thrilled to share them with you here so you can build the best antipasto platter ever.

INGREDIENTS

CHEESE. Pick at least three cheeses with varying flavors and textures. I like to use provolone, Parmigiano-Reggiano, and marinated mozzarella balls.

MEAT. I love to offer a selection of cured meats on my antipasto platter. For this board, I used Genoa salami, prosciutto, bresaola, coppa, and hard soppressata.

PICKLED VEGETABLES. I selected an assortment of pickled pepperoncini, pickled cherry peppers stuffed with prosciutto, and Roasted Red Peppers (page 30). Feel free to add others, such as pickled green beans or even Eggplant Caponata (page 26).

MARINATED VEGETABLES. Artichoke hearts, lupini beans, sun-dried tomatoes, and marinated mushrooms are all great choices, but feel free to choose others!

OLIVES. I used an assortment of red, green, and black oil-cured olives, but use any combination you'd like.

FRESH INGREDIENTS. When I can find them, I love to use ripe cherry tomatoes on the vine. They make for a beautiful presentation. I also like to scatter fresh oranges about. If you can find them with their leaves on, even better! Grapes would also be great here.

DRIED FRUIT. I used dried figs to fill in gaps on this antipasto board, but any other dried fruit, such as apricots or dates, would also work well.

CRACKERS. I used grissini, or long Italian breadsticks, but Rosemary Taralli (page 21) or other crackers would also be a great accompaniment.

GARNISH. Fresh herbs like rosemary, basil, or thyme make for a beautiful presentation.

How-To

BUILDING THE PLATTER

1. **Select a board.** The board does not need to be anything fancy and you don't need to spend a ton of money. I've found some of the best deals on boards at Home Goods and Home Sense, which are also great places to find Italian ingredients such as breadsticks and marinated or pickled vegetables. Get a board that's large enough to hold a good assortment of food. The one I use is 16 x 24 inches.

2. **Gather your ingredients.** Use the ingredients I've listed opposite as a starting point and feel free to tweak to your own liking. I try to follow this ratio when selecting items: 7 types of vegetables (pickled or marinated), 5 types of meat, 3 types of cheese, 2 to 3 types of olives, and 2 to 3 fruits or fresh vegetables.

3. **Pick a centerpiece.** I like to pick a large bowl and use that as a centerpiece around which to build the antipasto platter. For example, you can use a wooden bowl filled with fresh mozzarella balls.

4. **Stagger small bowls.** Fill a variety of smaller bowls with your pickled and marinated items and arrange them around the board.

5. **Place your cheeses.** I cut about half of each block of hard cheese and placed them on opposite sides with their tips pointing toward the centerpiece.

6. **Roll and place the meat.** Depending on the type of meat you're using, you can either roll it up (works well for salami), or shape into a flower or nest (works well for prosciutto). Place the meat around the board in various areas.

7. **Fill in any gaps.** Use your fruit and vegetables to fill in any gaps. If using dried figs, you may wish to cut them in half for an even better presentation.

8. **Garnish.** While garnishes are optional, they do add great color. I used rosemary, but parsley and/or basil would work well too.

9. **Serve!** I recommend building the antipasto platter before your guests arrive so you can just kick back and enjoy yourself. If making it ahead, cover the board in plastic wrap and place in the refrigerator, then remove 30 minutes before serving. If you're making this more than an hour or two in advance, hold off on adding the crackers or breadsticks until 30 minutes prior to serving. Consider serving with some Italian aperitivo cocktails, such as the Limoncello Spritz (page 234), Hugo Spritz (page 235), or White Peach Bellini (page 233).

SIP & FEAST TIPS

PASTA and GRAINS

For many, myself included, pasta is a source of comfort. Whether it's made with a simple marinara, a hearty ragu, or a velvety cream sauce, each dish has the power to soothe the soul. Some of these recipes excite the tastebuds with new and interesting flavors, while others serve up a sense of nostalgia for days gone by.

While looking through this chapter and selecting which recipes you want to try (I hope you try them all!), bear in mind that you can serve each of these as a pasta course before the main course, or as a meal itself. In Italy, pasta is almost always served in small portions as a precursor to the main course, while in the United States, we tend to consider pasta a main course with big heaping portions. As always, I encourage you to do what you want (as long as it includes saving your pasta water!). There have been many nights where we've made an entire meal out of a pasta dish, especially if it's more substantial, like Pappardelle with Braised Short Rib Ragu *(page 86)* *or Pasta alla Jimmy* *(page 69)**.*

WEEKNIGHT PASTA MARINARA

MAKES: 4 SERVINGS • PREP: 5 MINUTES • COOK: 20 MINUTES

Classic marinara sauce should never be difficult. Tomatoes, salt, garlic, olive oil, and some fresh basil are essentially all that's needed. No need to empty your spice cabinets for this one. In the time it takes to boil pasta, you can make a simple and delicious marinara whose taste rivals that of any restaurant, and certainly any shelf-stable sauce!

Pasta is one of the most common uses for marinara sauce, but as you go through this book you'll notice that this type of quick sauce is used for many other dishes, such as Stuffed Cubanelle Peppers (page 141), Stuffed Shells (page 90), and New York–Style Eggplant Parm (page 154). I suggest making a large batch (double or triple this recipe) and freezing the excess for whenever you need it.

INGREDIENTS

¼ cup (60 ml) extra virgin olive oil

6 cloves garlic, sliced

3 tablespoons (45 g) tomato paste

½ teaspoon crushed hot red pepper flakes, optional

¼ cup (60 ml) water

1 (28-ounce) can whole plum tomatoes, hand crushed or pulsed in a blender

1 pound (454 g) pasta of your choice

Salt and pepper, to taste

10 fresh basil leaves

INSTRUCTIONS

Bring a large pot of salted water to boil for the pasta.

Heat the olive oil and garlic in a large saucepan over medium heat. Once the garlic turns lightly golden, 2 to 3 minutes, add the tomato paste and cook for about 5 minutes, stirring frequently. Add the red pepper flakes toward the end of this cooking time, if using.

Add the water to loosen the paste and give it a stir. Add the plum tomatoes.

Cook for 5 to 10 minutes at a simmer. Meanwhile, cook the pasta to 1 minute less than al dente. Drain, reserving about 1 cup of the pasta water.

Taste-test the sauce and adjust the salt, pepper, and crushed red pepper levels if needed.

Remove half the sauce from the pan. Add the pasta to the remaining sauce in the pan and cook over medium-low heat, stirring to coat, for 1 minute or until al dente. If necessary, add a bit more sauce to get the sauce level just right. Add about ¼ cup of pasta water to loosen, if required.

Hand tear the basil leaves and add to the pasta right before serving. Serve with grated cheese and crusty Italian bread, if desired. Enjoy!

Since there are so few ingredients in this sauce, I recommend using the best quality tomatoes your budget allows.

If you opt for pulsing the tomatoes in a blender over hand crushing them, take care not to over-blend. This can add oxygen to the tomatoes and turn them orange.

The only herb I use for marinara is fresh basil. If you don't have fresh basil, you can omit it entirely. I do not recommend replacing it with dried basil, nor do I recommend using anything labeled "Italian seasoning."

Be sure to reserve your pasta water, as it is an essential part of this dish.

SIP & FEAST TIPS

RIGATONI WITH SUNDAY SAUCE AND MEATBALLS

MAKES: 6–8 SERVINGS • **PREP:** 20 MINUTES • **COOK:** 3 HOURS

While marinara sauce sits on the quick-and-fresh end of the spectrum, Sunday sauce, also known as "gravy," is situated on the long and rich end. With its brick-red color, deep and dark flavors, and proclivity to be served every Sunday in most Italian American households, this sauce is truly iconic and is the foundation for the quintessential Sunday dinner (see page 108).

There is no one way to make this sauce, and if you happen to be Italian American, or know Italian Americans, you have likely realized that the types of tomatoes, meat, herbs, and other ingredients vary, with the exact formula often kept close to the vest by nonnas far and wide.

This recipe is my own version of Sunday sauce, and each time I make it I change a little something about it. For example, this recipe includes meatballs, but sometimes I'll add Braciole (page 134), sausage, or pork ribs. In fact, this was the most challenging recipe for me to write, because I never actually use a recipe for Sunday sauce!

FOR THE SAUCE AND PASTA

- ½ cup (120 ml) extra virgin olive oil
- 1 large onion, finely diced
- 6 cloves garlic, sliced
- 1 (6-ounce) can tomato paste
- 4 (28-ounce) cans plum tomatoes, hand crushed or pulsed in a blender
- Salt and pepper, to taste
- 1 to 2 teaspoons granulated sugar, optional
- 1 pound (454 g) pasta of your choice

FOR THE MEATBALLS

- 1 pound (454 g) ground chuck
- 1 pound (454 g) ground pork
- 2 teaspoons kosher salt
- ½ teaspoon ground black pepper
- 1½ cups (150 g) plain breadcrumbs
- ¾ cup (68 g) grated Parmigiano-Reggiano cheese
- ½ cup minced flat-leaf Italian parsley
- 3 cloves garlic, grated or finely minced to form a paste
- 2 to 3 large eggs, beaten

FOR THE SAUCE

Coat the bottom of a large heavy pot with the olive oil and sauté the onion over medium-low heat until translucent, 5 to 7 minutes. Add the garlic and cook until golden and fragrant, 2 to 3 minutes.

Add the tomato paste and cook for 5 minutes, spreading the paste around with a wooden spoon. Add a splash of water if the paste starts to burn.

Add the plum tomatoes and salt and pepper to taste. Stir the sauce until incorporated, then reduce the heat to low and partially cover. Cook, stirring every so often to avoid sticking, for at least 2½ hours, but the longer the better. Taste-test and add the sugar as needed to counter the acidity of the tomatoes.

FOR THE MEATBALLS

Preheat the oven to 375°F and set the rack to the middle level.

Combine the beef and ground pork in a large mixing bowl and season with the salt and pepper.

Add the breadcrumbs, cheese, parsley, and garlic. Add 2 of the eggs and gently mix everything together. If the mixture is too dry, add 1 more egg to the mix.

With wet hands, roll approximately 2-inch-diameter meatballs, then place on a wire rack set on a sheet pan. Bake for 25 to 30 minutes or until brown.

Place the browned meatballs in the sauce and cook for a minimum of 1 hour on low heat to allow the meatballs to absorb the flavor and braise in the sauce.

FOR THE PASTA

Right before the sauce is ready to eat, bring a large pot of salted water to boil and cook the pasta to al dente.

When the pasta is cooked, drain, and place in a serving bowl. Toss with the sauce to coat.

It is very important to stir the sauce occasionally to prevent it from sticking to the sides of the pot. If you've seen Goodfellas*, you'll remember Henry Hill yelling at his brother to not let the sauce stick, and it was 100% a valid concern. Gas burners tend to do a better job than electric ranges when it comes to preventing sticking. If sticking is a concern, you can also make the sauce in a large, covered Dutch oven in a 275°F oven.*

Feel free to add other meat to your Sunday sauce in addition to the meatballs. Country ribs, braciole, and pork neck bones are all great, or try using the T-bone left over from a steak.

PASTA E PISELLI

MAKES: 4 SERVINGS • **PREP:** 5 MINUTES • **COOK:** 35 MINUTES

There is something so comforting about pasta and peas. The sweetness of the peas paired with the creamy, starchy pasta is a winning combination, and for many of us, this dish is incredibly nostalgic and harkens back to a simpler time.

Since it's made with ingredients you likely have on hand (frozen peas, onions, and pasta), this recipe is perfect for nights when you can't get to the grocery store but still want something good. Traditionally this recipe is made with canned peas, but I like to use frozen. If you want to use canned instead, by all means go for it.

Since this version contains no meat, it's a great option for vegetarians and a true staple for Lenten Fridays!

INGREDIENTS

½ cup (120 ml) extra virgin olive oil, plus more for drizzling

1 large onion, finely diced

½ teaspoon crushed hot red pepper flakes

4 cups (960 ml) water, plus more if needed

1 pound (454 g) frozen peas

1 teaspoon fine sea salt, plus more to taste

1 pound (454 g) ditalini or other small pasta shape

1 cup (90 g) grated pecorino Romano cheese, plus more for serving

Salt and pepper, to taste

INSTRUCTIONS

Heat a large pot or pan over a touch less than medium heat and add the olive oil and onion. Cook the onion, stirring occasionally, until very soft and translucent, about 10 minutes, then add the red pepper flakes and cook for another 30 seconds.

Add the water, peas, and salt and bring to a boil. Once boiling, mash some of the peas with a wooden spoon.

Add the pasta and turn the heat down to medium. Cook the pasta at a moderate simmer until al dente. Make sure to stir frequently to avoid sticking, and add more water if the pot begins to dry out.

When satisfied with the consistency and the pasta has reached al dente, remove the pot from the heat and mix in the cheese. Taste-test and season with salt and black pepper. If the pasta is at all dry, add extra water to loosen it up.

Serve in bowls with a drizzle of extra virgin olive oil and a generous amount of grated pecorino Romano. Enjoy!

Feel free to add any ingredients you'd like to your pasta e piselli. Garlic, shallots, pancetta, fresh herbs, or anchovies would all be great, as would chicken stock in place of the water. If you prefer to use Parmigiano-Reggiano instead of pecorino Romano, you can do that too!

Be sure to stir frequently and add more water as needed to avoid sticking. If a soupier consistency is desired, just use more water.

SPAGHETTI ALLA NERANO

MAKES: 4–6 SERVINGS • **PREP:** 10 MINUTES • **COOK:** 35 MINUTES

Growing up, this dish was a regular in my home. My grandma would make it often and always called it "fried zucchini pasta." I can still remember coming in for dinner after playing soccer or basketball all day, sweaty and starving, and she'd place a bowl of this in front of me and tell me to eat. As if I needed any coaxing!

This dish hails from the beach town of Nerano in southern Italy, where it is typically made with provolone del Monaco. But since that cheese is difficult to procure here in the US, I opt for caciocavallo cheese, which can be found in most Italian grocery stores in the New York metropolitan area. If you cannot find caciocavallo, you can definitely use good-quality mild provolone and it will still be wonderful.

This is the perfect simple pasta for summer nights or anytime you have an abundance of zucchini!

FOR THE FRIED ZUCCHINI

½ cup (120 ml) olive oil, for frying

5 small to medium zucchini, sliced into disks about ⅛ inch (4 mm) thick

2 teaspoons kosher salt

FOR THE PASTA

1 pound (454 g) spaghetti

3 tablespoons (45 ml) extra virgin olive oil

4 cloves garlic

1 tablespoon (14 g) butter

1¼ cups (115 g) grated caciocavallo cheese, or provolone or pecorino Romano cheese, plus more for serving

Salt and pepper, to taste

¼ cup packed basil leaves, chopped

FOR THE FRIED ZUCCHINI

Heat the olive oil in a large frying pan over medium heat. Working in batches, fry the zucchini in the oil until golden brown, about 3 minutes per side, then place in a large pan lined with paper towels. Sprinkle salt onto the zucchini right after frying each batch. You can also use multiple pans to cook a few batches at once and speed up the cooking process.

FOR THE PASTA

Bring a large pot of salted water to boil and cook the spaghetti until 1 to 2 minutes less than al dente. Drain, reserving about 2 cups (480 ml) of the pasta water.

Meanwhile, heat the olive oil in a large pan over medium-low heat. Add the garlic and sauté until golden, 1 to 2 minutes. Once golden, remove and discard the garlic cloves, or save them for another use.

Add the butter, a ladle of pasta water, and half of the zucchini to the pan and bring to a simmer. Mash the zucchini with a wooden spoon on the side of the pan to create a loose zucchini sauce. Add the pasta to the pan and continue cooking for 1 to 2 minutes or until al dente.

Turn off the heat and add the cheese. Toss to emulsify until a creamy sauce is formed. If it's too dry, add a few more tablespoons of pasta water at a time, tossing after each addition, until the consistency is just right.

Taste-test and make any final adjustments to the salt and pepper, then add the basil. Top each portion with some of the remaining zucchini rounds, and serve right away with more grated cheese on the side.

Use the smallest zucchini you can find for this dish. Not only do they taste better, but they have fewer seeds and less water and are more tender.

To prevent the cheese from clumping, take the pan off the heat, then toss the pasta with the cheese. Adding a touch of cooled-down pasta water or even cold water will help loosen the cheese as well.

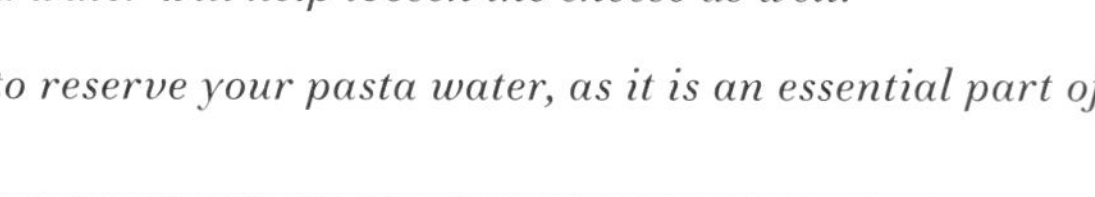

Be sure to reserve your pasta water, as it is an essential part of this dish.

FETTUCCINE WITH CHERRY TOMATO BUTTER SAUCE

MAKES: 4–6 SERVINGS • **PREP:** 5 MINUTES • **COOK:** 35 MINUTES

There's nothing simpler than pasta with a tomato and butter sauce, especially for weeknights when you're short on time but do not want to compromise on flavor. The combination of tomatoes and butter is pure magic, and when tossed with the starchy pasta water, the sauce takes on a velvety texture that is out of this world.

This recipe was inspired by Italian culinary queen Marcella Hazan's tomato butter sauce, but with a few tweaks. Her recipe calls for crushed tomatoes, and she leaves the onion whole so it can be removed after cooking. Our version opts for cherry tomatoes and diced onion because we like a little extra texture.

This dish is proof that sometimes the best things are the simplest!

INGREDIENTS

8 tablespoons (113 g) butter

1 medium onion, finely diced

36 ounces (1 kg) cherry tomatoes, halved

1 teaspoon kosher salt, plus more to taste

1 pound (454 g) fettuccine, or other long pasta, such as linguine

Black pepper, to taste

¼ cup minced flat-leaf Italian parsley

¼ cup packed basil, hand torn

Grated parmesan cheese, to taste

INSTRUCTIONS

Heat the butter in a large saucepan over medium-low heat and sauté the onion until soft, about 5 minutes, then add the tomatoes. Season the tomatoes with a teaspoon of kosher salt.

Cook the sauce over medium heat, stirring frequently, for 30 to 35 minutes, until the cherry tomatoes have burst and softened and the butter has completely blended in with the tomatoes. Lower the heat if needed to prevent scorching.

Meanwhile, bring a large pot of salted water to boil. When the sauce is almost to your liking, begin cooking the fettuccine. A few minutes before the pasta finishes cooking, remove 1 cup of pasta water and add it to the sauce and stir to combine. Continue to cook the sauce over medium heat. Drain the pasta when it is 1 minute shy of al dente, reserving another 1 cup (240 ml) of the pasta water.

Add the pasta to the sauce and toss to coat. Cook until the pasta is just al dente, then turn off the heat and season to taste with salt and pepper. Add the herbs and toss once more. If the pasta is at all dry, add more of the reserved pasta water a little at a time to loosen it up. Serve with grated parmesan cheese.

I used 36 ounces, or 1 kg, of cherry tomatoes, but feel free to add more if you'd like more sauce. You can even add some canned crushed tomatoes.

Be sure to save your pasta water! It helps to reconstitute the sauce if it becomes too dry. Start by adding a little at a time to prevent the pasta from becoming too watery.

I love this dish with fresh basil and parsley at the end. If you can't find fresh herbs, you can omit them. I do not recommend using dried herbs for this recipe.

SIP & FEAST TIPS

BLACKENED CHICKEN ALFREDO PASTA

MAKES: 4 SERVINGS • PREP: 5 MINUTES • COOK: 25 MINUTES

Purists will tell you that adding chicken to pasta is a cardinal sin, as is adding cream (or garlic) to Alfredo sauce. It is my opinion that those who feel that way have never eaten chicken Alfredo pasta.

While this recipe certainly deviates from traditional Alfredo, it's equally delicious, if not better, and is packed with wonderful flavor. And besides, when it comes to cooking, rules are meant to be broken.

I use a blackened spice for the chicken. If you can't find this ingredient, you can use Cajun seasoning, which may have a bit more heat. You can also use salt and pepper, and it will still be great!

FOR THE CHICKEN

- 1 pound (454 g) thin-sliced chicken cutlets
- 2½ teaspoons blackened spice, optional, or 1 teaspoon kosher salt and ½ teaspoon ground black pepper
- 1 tablespoon (15 ml) extra virgin olive oil
- 1 tablespoon (14 g) butter

FOR THE PASTA

- 8 ounces (227 g) egg fettuccine or egg pappardelle
- 7 tablespoons (98 g) butter
- 3 cloves garlic, minced
- 1¼ cups (113 g) grated Parmigiano-Reggiano cheese, plus more for serving
- 1¼ cups (300 ml) heavy cream
- Salt and pepper, to taste
- 3 tablespoons minced flat-leaf Italian parsley

INSTRUCTIONS

Bring a large pot of salted water to boil.

FOR THE CHICKEN

Dry the chicken with paper towels, then season with the blackened spice on both sides.

Heat a large stainless steel or cast iron frying pan over medium heat and wait 3 minutes. Coat the pan with the olive oil and add the chicken. After 2 minutes add the butter. Cook for 1 minute more, then flip and cook for about 3 minutes on the other side. Place the cooked chicken on a cutting board and cover with tented foil.

FOR THE PASTA

Add the pasta to the boiling water and cook to al dente.

While the pasta is cooking, heat a large, clean pan over medium-low heat and add the butter and garlic. Cook the garlic for 2 minutes or until golden, then add the cheese and cream and bring to a simmer, stirring occasionally. The sauce will begin to thicken after a couple of minutes of simmering.

Drain the pasta, reserving about 1 cup (240 ml) of the pasta water. Add the pasta to the sauce and mix or toss to coat. If the pasta is too dry, add some of the reserved pasta water a little at a time to get a perfect consistency.

Remove the pan from the heat. Season with salt and pepper to taste and add the parsley. Cut the chicken into slices and use it to top each individual serving, or mix it straight into the pasta in the pan. Serve immediately with grated Parmigiano-Reggiano on the side.

To save money, buy whole chicken breasts and fillet them yourself. Pound them to about ½ inch thick for best results and faster cooking. This also creates maximum surface area for the blackened seasoning. Be sure to take the time to dry the cutlets with paper towels before seasoning.

Be sure to save your pasta water since it is a key ingredient in this dish. It helps to emulsify the sauce and can be used to reconstitute a sauce that's dried out.

I recommend serving this dish right away. As with most cream sauces, it's best when fresh.

PASTA ALLA JIMMY

MAKES: 4–6 SERVINGS • **PREP:** 10 MINUTES • **COOK:** 25 MINUTES

If you've ever heard of a "garbage pizza," this is similar, but in pasta form. This is a dish I used to make once a week when the kids were little, and everyone loved it. Every weekend Tara would do our grocery shopping at Fairway Market in Plainview, New York, and they had the most fantastic olive bar. There she'd pick up Peppadew peppers, olives, roasted garlic, and marinated butter beans. She'd also pick up their chicken sausage and I'd combine all of it together with pasta. The kids loved it, and Tara would take it with her to work to have for lunch, where a friend and coworker lovingly dubbed it "Pasta alla Jimmy."

While these are the ingredients I like to use, I encourage you to get creative—use some or all of these, or add in a few of your own!

INGREDIENTS

- 5 tablespoons (75 ml) extra virgin olive oil, divided
- 1 pound (454 g) bulk Italian sausage
- 1 pound (454 g) rigatoni or paccheri
- 1 (15-ounce) can butter beans, drained
- 1 cup (140 g) olives, pitted and coarsely chopped
- 1 cup (140 g) coarsely chopped Peppadew peppers
- 20 cloves roasted garlic
- ½ teaspoon crushed hot red pepper flakes
- Salt and pepper, to taste
- ½ cup (45 g) grated pecorino Romano cheese, plus more for serving
- ¼ cup minced flat-leaf Italian parsley

INSTRUCTIONS

Bring a large pot of salted water to boil.

Heat 2 tablespoons of the olive oil in a large saucepan over medium heat. Once shimmering, add the sausage. Cook the sausage until browned and break it up into small pieces.

Add the pasta to the boiling water and cook to 1 minute less than al dente.

Meanwhile, add the remaining 3 tablespoons of olive oil, the butter beans, olives, Peppadew peppers, roasted garlic, and red pepper flakes to the pan and mix to combine.

Remove 1 cup (240 ml) of pasta water and add to the pan, and continue to simmer while the pasta finishes cooking.

When the pasta is almost al dente, drain, reserving about 1 cup (240 ml) more pasta water. Add the pasta to the sauce and stir quickly. Mix well or toss to emulsify. Once the pasta reaches al dente, remove the pan from the heat.

Taste and adjust the salt and pepper if required. Mix in the cheese and parsley. Add more pasta water, a bit at a time, to get the perfect consistency. Serve with extra pecorino on the side.

If you cannot find bulk Italian sausage, simply buy sausage links, cut a slit down the middle, and remove the sausage from its casing.

Some great olive choices for this dish include Gaeta, Sicilian Castelvetrano, or Greek kalamata.

Roasting the garlic ahead of time allows this recipe to be completed in about 30 minutes. I like to roast 20 heads at a time, freeze, and save for later use. You can often find roasted garlic at the olive bar in your local grocery store, which is where we get the olives and Peppadews.

Since there are several salty ingredients in this dish, you will likely not need much additional salt.

Be sure to reserve your pasta water, as it is an essential part of this dish.

LINGUINE WITH CANNED CLAMS

MAKES: 4–6 SERVINGS • **PREP:** 10 MINUTES • **COOK:** 20 MINUTES

More often than not I find myself craving linguine with clam sauce, and often late at night! I always keep some canned clams in my pantry so I can easily satisfy my craving, no matter the time.

Canned seafood is a wonderful staple to keep on hand in your pantry, and I typically keep several cans of baby clams, clam juice, sardines, oil-packed tuna, and anchovies on hand for when I want to make a simple meal without running to the grocery store.

While this recipe lists the seasoned breadcrumbs as optional, I highly recommend using them—they really take the dish over the top!

FOR THE SEASONED BREADCRUMBS (OPTIONAL)

- 5 slices day-old bread, crusts removed, or 1 cup store-bought plain breadcrumbs
- 3 tablespoons minced flat-leaf Italian parsley
- ½ clove garlic, minced
- ½ teaspoon kosher salt
- 3 tablespoons (45 ml) extra virgin olive oil

FOR THE CLAM SAUCE

- 3 (10-ounce) cans baby clams (see notes opposite)
- 5 tablespoons (75 ml) extra virgin olive oil
- 7 cloves garlic, sliced
- 5 anchovy fillets
- 1 pound (454 g) linguine
- ¼ teaspoon crushed hot red pepper flakes
- ½ cup (120 ml) dry white wine
- ¼ cup minced flat-leaf Italian parsley
- 2 tablespoons (28 g) butter, cubed
- Salt and pepper, to taste

FOR THE SEASONED BREADCRUMBS

In a food processor, pulse the bread along with the parsley, garlic, salt, and olive oil.

Heat a large frying pan over medium heat and add the breadcrumb mixture to the pan. Cook, stirring frequently, until the breadcrumbs turn golden, 5 to 7 minutes.

FOR THE CLAM SAUCE

Bring a large pot of salted water to a boil.

Separate the canned baby clams from their juice, reserving both.

Heat a large frying pan over medium-low heat and add the olive oil, garlic, and anchovies. Cook until the garlic is golden and the anchovies dissolve, about 3 minutes.

Meanwhile, add the linguine to the boiling water and cook to 1 minute less than al dente.

Add the red pepper flakes to the pan with the garlic and anchovies and cook for another 30 seconds. Add the wine and turn the heat up to medium-high. Cook the wine for 2 to 3 minutes or until it slightly reduces, then add the reserved clam juice.

Turn the heat down to medium-low, add the baby clams to the pan, and mix well.

Drain the linguine, reserving about 2 cups (480 ml) of the pasta water. Add the linguine to the pan and toss or mix with tongs to emulsify the sauce. Cook the pasta with the sauce for 1 minute or until the pasta just reaches al dente. If the pasta is dry, add a little reserved pasta water at a time until the pasta has plenty of sauce.

Turn the heat off and add the parsley and butter. Mix well then taste-test. Adjust the salt and pepper levels, if required. Serve in bowls with the seasoned breadcrumbs on the side, if using.

Three 10-ounce cans of baby clams will yield approximately 18 ounces of clam juice. If needed, use extra store-bought clam juice or more pasta water to make up the difference.

If you don't have day-old bread or hard bread, simply toast fresh pieces of bread in a 350°F oven for 10 to 15 minutes to dry them out.

Clams, anchovies, and pasta water are inherently salty, so I don't add any extra salt. Taste-test the sauce and adjust the salt to suit your taste.

Be sure to reserve your pasta water, as it is an essential part of this dish.

LEMON-GARLIC SHRIMP PASTA

MAKES: 4–6 SERVINGS • **PREP:** 10 MINUTES • **BRINE:** 10 MINUTES • **COOK:** 20 MINUTES

This is the perfect pasta to make when you want to make an impression with minimal effort! The combination of the buttery, garlicky sauce with parsley, lemon juice, and lemon zest and the plump shrimp is amazing, especially when tossed together with the al dente pasta.

This is a recipe I turn to again and again, especially on busy weeknights, because it can be ready in about 30 minutes. Keeping a bag of frozen shrimp in your freezer comes in very handy for dishes like this one.

FOR THE BRINED SHRIMP

1½ pounds (680 g) large shrimp (21–25 ct.), shelled and deveined

½ teaspoon baking soda

½ teaspoon kosher salt

¼ teaspoon ground black pepper

¼ teaspoon crushed hot red pepper flakes

FOR THE PASTA

1 pound (454 g) spaghetti

⅓ cup (80 ml) extra virgin olive oil, plus more as needed

10 cloves garlic, sliced

5 tablespoons (70 g) butter

¼ cup minced flat-leaf Italian parsley

1 large lemon, zested and juiced

Salt and pepper, to taste

FOR THE BRINED SHRIMP

Place the shrimp and all the brining ingredients into a large bowl and mix well. Let rest 10 minutes before sautéing.

FOR THE PASTA

Bring a large pot of salted water to boil and cook the pasta to 1 minute less than al dente.

Meanwhile, heat the olive oil in a large frying pan over medium heat. Once shimmering, add the shrimp in one layer (work in batches, if necessary), and sauté for about 3 minutes or until cooked through and the shrimp are firm and pink. Remove the shrimp to a plate and cover with tented foil to keep warm.

Add the garlic to the pan and sauté it for 2 to 3 minutes or until lightly golden. If the pan is dry, add a touch more olive oil.

Drain the pasta, reserving about 2 cups (480 ml) of the pasta water. Add ½ cup of pasta water to the pan along with the butter and the almost-cooked pasta. Cook for 1 minute, tossing to coat well so the sauce absorbs and clings to the pasta. Add the cooked shrimp, parsley, and lemon zest and juice and toss to mix again.

Turn off the heat and taste-test. Make any final adjustments to the salt, black pepper, and red pepper flakes. If the pasta is too dry, add a few more ounces of pasta water. Serve immediately.

Frozen shrimp are a great ingredient to keep on hand so you can quickly throw together a dish like this in a pinch. Just be sure the shrimp are completely thawed before using.

Brining the shrimp with baking soda helps to keep them plump. While you can skip this step, I recommend taking the extra 10 minutes for best results.

Be sure to reserve your pasta water, as it is an essential part of this dish.

SIP & FEAST TIPS

SHRIMP AND LINGUINE FRA DIAVOLO

MAKES: 4–6 SERVINGS • PREP: 15 MINUTES • BRINE: 10 MINUTES • COOK: 20 MINUTES

Growing up on Long Island, shrimp fra diavolo was a favorite of mine and was the first dish I ordered off the "grown-up menu." It's almost always served with linguine, and sometimes a few clams or mussels for good measure.

Fra diavolo is Italian for "from the devil" or "brother devil," and some people believe the dish was named for a Neapolitan guerrilla leader. However, the *New York Times* claims this dish was created in the United States by Italian immigrants, which would explain why it's available at nearly every Italian American restaurant in the New York metropolitan area. It's incredibly easy to make, delicious, perfectly spicy, and a not-so-secret ingredient, brandy, amps up the flavor even more!

FOR THE SHRIMP

- 1½ pounds (680 g) extra-large shrimp (26 count or larger), shelled and deveined
- 1 teaspoon paprika, for color, optional
- 1 teaspoon kosher salt
- 1 teaspoon crushed hot red pepper flakes
- ½ teaspoon baking soda
- ¼ cup (60 ml) extra virgin olive oil, divided

FOR THE PASTA

- ¼ cup (60 ml) extra virgin olive oil
- 3 anchovy fillets
- 8 cloves garlic, sliced
- 1 teaspoon crushed hot red pepper flakes, plus more to taste
- ½ cup (120 ml) dry white wine
- 1 (28-ounce) can plum tomatoes, hand crushed or pulsed in a blender
- ½ teaspoon dried oregano
- Salt and pepper, to taste
- 1 pound (454 g) linguine
- 3 tablespoons (45 ml) brandy, optional
- ¼ cup minced flat-leaf Italian parsley

FOR THE SHRIMP

Place the shrimp, paprika, salt, red pepper flakes, baking soda, and 2 tablespoons of the olive oil into a large bowl and mix well to coat. Set aside for at least 10 minutes before sautéing.

Heat the remaining 2 tablespoons of olive oil in a large frying pan over medium-high heat. Once shimmering, add the shrimp, working in batches if necessary to avoid overcrowding the pan, and cook for 60 to 90 seconds per side or until almost cooked. Place the seared shrimp on a plate and cover with tented foil.

FOR THE PASTA

Bring a large pot of salted water to boil.

Heat the same pan you used for the shrimp over medium heat and add the olive oil, anchovies, and garlic. Mash the anchovies with a spoon to help them dissolve. Once the garlic is golden, 2 to 3 minutes, add the red pepper flakes and cook for another 30 seconds.

Add the wine and turn the heat to high. With a wooden spoon, scrape the bottom of the pan to dislodge any brown bits. Once the wine reduces by half, add the tomatoes and bring to a lively simmer. Add the oregano and season with a touch of salt and pepper to taste if needed. Turn the heat down and keep the sauce on a low simmer.

Add the pasta to the boiling water and cook it to 1 minute less than al dente. A few minutes before the pasta is done, add the brandy to the sauce, if using. When the pasta is almost al dente, drain, reserving about 2 cups (480 ml) of the pasta water.

Add the pasta and shrimp to the pan and toss or mix to coat.

If the pasta is too dry, add some of the reserved pasta water. Once the pasta is al dente, remove the pan from the heat and taste the sauce. Season with salt and pepper if required, add the parsley, then serve immediately.

Shrimp fra diavolo is a spicy dish, but if you prefer it less spicy, decrease the amount of crushed red pepper. If you like things hot, add as much as you'd like and serve more on the side for those who want even more!

Brining the shrimp for 10 minutes with baking soda helps to keep them plump. While you can skip this step, I recommend taking the extra 10 minutes for best results.

Be sure to reserve your pasta water, as it is an essential part of this dish.

Use the ingredients that are available to you. If you can't find cremini mushrooms, use white button mushrooms; if you can't find pecorino Romano, use Parmigiano-Reggiano or grana Padano, and so on.

Nutmeg is a strong spice and can be overpowering, so start by adding just a pinch and serve more on the side for those who'd like more.

Be sure to reserve your pasta water, as it is an essential part of this dish.

PASTA ALLA NORCINA

MAKES: 6–8 SERVINGS • **PREP:** 10 MINUTES • **COOK:** 25 MINUTES

Pasta alla Norcina may be the most underrated pasta ever. Underrated because with a few exceptions, I have not seen this on the menu of Italian restaurants here in New York, and I think it deserves to be! Perhaps it's because this dish hails from the city of Norcia in Italy's Umbria region, while most of the Italian immigrants who came to the United States (my ancestors included) were from southern Italy and Sicily.

Traditionally, pasta alla Norcina features a pork sausage made in Norcia using a combination of white wine and nutmeg. It's a bit different from the typical fennel pork sausage available here in the US. In addition to this local sausage, the dish is also typically topped with a shaving of black truffles, which are also foraged in Norcia.

My attempt here is to deviate slightly from tradition and use ingredients that are more widely accessible and economical, while hopefully still maintaining the overall integrity of the dish. I use bulk mild pork sausage and cremini mushrooms, along with some nutmeg, white wine, and heavy cream. Some recipes use ricotta instead of cream. In my opinion, cream is much better.

The result is quite possibly the creamiest, most velvety, most flavorful pasta you'll ever eat.

INGREDIENTS

¼ cup (60 ml) extra virgin olive oil

1 pound (454 g) bulk mild Italian sausage

8 ounces (226 g) cremini mushrooms, diced

1 small onion, diced

3 cloves garlic, smashed

½ cup (120 ml) dry white wine

1 pound (454 g) paccheri, rigatoni, or other tubular pasta

1½ cups (360 ml) heavy cream

¾ cup (68 g) grated pecorino Romano cheese, plus more for serving

1 pinch ground nutmeg

Salt and pepper, to taste

INSTRUCTIONS

Bring a large pot of salted water to boil.

Heat a large pan over medium heat and add the olive oil and sausage. Brown the sausage, stirring occasionally, for 5 to 7 minutes, then make some room in the pan, add the mushrooms, and continue to cook until they brown as well, 5 to 7 minutes.

Once the sausage and mushrooms are brown, add the onion and garlic. After 2 minutes remove the garlic from the pan and discard or save for another use. Continue cooking for a few more minutes until the onion softens.

Turn the heat to medium-high and add the wine. Cook for a minute to reduce the wine by about half while gently scraping the bottom of the pan with a wooden spoon to dislodge the brown bits.

Add the pasta to the boiling water and begin cooking to 1 minute less than al dente. Add the cream to the sauce and bring it to a simmer while stirring. Once simmering, turn the heat down to low.

When the pasta is almost al dente, drain, reserving about 2 cups (480 ml) of the pasta water. Add the pasta to the sauce and toss or mix to coat. Turn the heat to medium and add a bit of pasta water if needed to loosen the sauce. Continue to cook, stirring frequently, until the pasta is al dente.

Remove the pan from the heat and add the pecorino, mix well, and taste-test. Season with a good amount of pepper, a pinch of nutmeg, and salt to taste. Serve with grated pecorino.

SPICY SAUSAGE MAFALDINE

MAKES: 6–8 SERVINGS • **PREP:** 15 MINUTES • **COOK:** 1 HOUR, 30 MINUTES

If you like a little spice in your life, this is the dish for you! The ragu combines hot Italian sausage and Calabrian chili paste in a tomato-red wine sauce that's tossed with mafaldine and finished with plenty of pecorino Romano.

I chose to use mafaldine pasta here because its wavy edges are perfect for capturing bits of the sausage ragu. Since this pasta shape can be harder to find, you can use pappardelle or rigatoni in its place. As always, you have the option to make this as spicy as you'd like, so feel free to add more Calabrian chili paste, or omit it entirely, depending on your taste.

INGREDIENTS

- 2 tablespoons (30 ml) extra virgin olive oil
- 6 ounces (170 g) pancetta, diced
- 1½ pounds (680 g) bulk hot Italian sausage
- 1 medium white onion, finely diced
- 2 large carrots, finely diced
- 2 celery ribs, finely diced
- Salt, to taste
- ¼ cup (60 g) tomato paste
- 1 cup (240 ml) dry red wine
- 2 (28-ounce) cans plum tomatoes, hand crushed or pulsed in a blender
- 1 pound (454 g) mafaldine, pappardelle, or rigatoni
- Calabrian chili paste, to taste
- ½ cup (45 g) grated pecorino Romano cheese, plus more for serving

INSTRUCTIONS

Heat the olive oil in a large Dutch oven or heavy-bottomed pot over medium heat and add the pancetta. Sauté the pancetta for 7 to 10 minutes or until most of the fat has rendered.

Add the sausage to the pot and cook for 7 to 10 minutes, breaking it up with a wooden spoon or meat masher, until it begins to brown. Remove the sausage and pancetta with a slotted spoon (leaving the fat in the pot), place on a plate, and set aside.

Add the onion, carrots, celery, and a pinch of salt to the pot and cook for 15 minutes or until very soft, stirring occasionally. If the vegetables start to burn, lower the heat and/or add a splash of water. Return the sausage to the pot and add the tomato paste. Cook for 3 minutes, mixing well to combine.

Add the wine and turn the heat to high. Once boiling, use a wooden spoon to gently scrape the bottom of the pot to dislodge any brown bits. Add the tomatoes and stir to combine. Bring the sauce to a boil, then turn the heat down and simmer for 45 minutes, partially covered.

When the simmering time is nearly finished, bring a pot of salted water to boil and cook the mafaldine to 1 minute less than al dente. Drain, reserving about 1 cup (240 ml) of the pasta water.

Test the ragu and if it isn't spicy enough, add Calabrian chili paste to taste. Season with salt as needed.

Transfer half of the ragu to a large pan over medium heat. Add the cooked pasta and toss to coat. If needed, add a splash of the reserved pasta water to loosen it up. Once the pasta reaches al dente, remove the pan from the heat. Add the cheese and mix well. Add a bit more of the ragu and pasta water as needed, then serve with more cheese. The remaining ragu can be served in a gravy bowl or saved for another occasion.

For even more flavor, make the ragu 24 hours in advance and refrigerate overnight. This will also allow you to remove some of the fat that will rise to the top after being chilled.

Feel free to adjust the ingredients to suit your taste. If you prefer less spice, omit the Calabrian chili paste.

Be sure to reserve your pasta water, as it's an essential part of this dish.

If using fresh pasta, you will not need to add the heavy cream, unless you want to. Dried pasta tends to do better with heavy cream.

For maximum flavor and easier fat removal, make the Bolognese a day ahead and allow it to rest in the refrigerator overnight.

Nutmeg can be overpowering if too much of it is used, so use it sparingly and serve extra on the side so others can add it to their taste.

Be sure to reserve your pasta water, as it is an essential part of this dish.

JIM'S BOLOGNESE

MAKES: 6–8 SERVINGS • **PREP:** 15 MINUTES • **COOK:** 4 HOURS, 45 MINUTES

If you visit our website, you'll find a traditional Bolognese recipe that is nearly identical to the one set forth by the Bologna Chamber of Commerce. While traditional Bolognese is wonderful, I've found that adding a few nontraditional ingredients elevates the flavor of this dish in a very big way.

Bolognese is particularly good with pappardelle or tagliatelle, but you can also make it with rigatoni or paccheri. Since it takes several hours to cook, it's especially good on a Sunday alongside some garlicky sautéed greens and a crusty loaf of Italian bread.

INGREDIENTS

¼ pound (114 g) pancetta, diced

¾ pound (340 g) ground pork

¾ pound (340 g) ground chuck

2 celery ribs, finely diced

1 large carrot, finely diced

1 medium onion, finely diced

3 anchovy fillets

1 cup (240 ml) dry red wine

2 (28-ounce) cans plum tomatoes, hand crushed or pulsed in a blender

1 cup (240 ml) low-sodium beef stock

½ cup (120 ml) milk, divided

1 large (2-3 inches) Parmigiano-Reggiano cheese rind

2 large bay leaves

¼ cup (60 ml) heavy cream, optional

1 pound (454 g) pappardelle or tagliatelle

Salt and pepper, to taste

1 pinch ground nutmeg, plus more to taste

Grated Parmigiano-Reggiano cheese, for serving

INSTRUCTIONS

Preheat the oven to 300°F and set the racks to accommodate a Dutch oven and its lid.

Heat a large Dutch oven or ovenproof heavy pot over medium heat and add the pancetta. Cook the pancetta until most of the fat has rendered, 7 to 10 minutes, stirring occasionally.

Add the ground pork and beef and sauté until brown, 7 to 10 minutes, while breaking it up with a wooden spoon or meat masher. Once browned, use a slotted spoon to remove the ground meat and pancetta to a plate and set aside. Add the celery, carrot, onion, and anchovies to the pot along with a pinch of salt, and sauté until very soft, 12 to 15 minutes. If they start to burn, lower the heat and/or add a splash of water.

Add the meat back to the pot along with the wine and turn the heat to high. With a wooden spoon, scrape the bottom of the pot to dislodge any brown bits. Once the wine reduces, add the tomatoes, beef stock, ¼ cup of the milk, the Parmigiano-Reggiano rind, and bay leaves and bring to a boil.

Once boiling, turn off the heat and cover. Place the pot in the oven and cook for 3 hours. After 3 hours, remove the lid and cook for another 30 minutes.

After 3½ hours the fat from the meat and the pancetta will float to the top and the ragu will have thickened somewhat. Degrease the pot with a spoon or paper towels, leaving some of the fat. Add the remaining ¼ cup milk and the cream, if using, and stir to combine. Cook on the stovetop at a simmer for 15 to 30 minutes more. Taste the sauce and add salt and pepper as needed. Remove and discard the cheese rind and bay leaves.

Bring a large pot of salted water to boil and cook the pappardelle until 1 minute less than al dente. Drain, reserving about 2 cups (480 ml) of the pasta water.

To sauce the pasta, combine 2 cups of the ragu and ½ cup of pasta water in a pan over medium-low heat, then add the almost-cooked pasta and cook for 1 to 2 minutes so that the pasta can absorb the sauce. Add extra sauce as required. Add a pinch of nutmeg and serve with grated Parmigiano-Reggiano.

ORECCHIETTE WITH SAUSAGE AND BROCCOLI RABE

MAKES: 6–8 SERVINGS • PREP: 10 MINUTES • COOK: 35 MINUTES

There are some things that are greater than the sum of their parts, and orecchiette, sausage, and broccoli rabe is a prime example! This is one of my favorite dishes of all time, one my family asks me to make on repeat, and one that's fairly easy to make. In fact, this was one of the first dishes our son James learned how to make.

We like things spicy in our home, so we usually add a few more sliced cherry peppers to the dish at the very end, but that's completely optional!

INGREDIENTS

1 pound (454 g) broccoli rabe, bottom 1 inch of stems trimmed, chopped into 2-inch pieces

1½ pounds (680 g) bulk sweet Italian sausage

1 pound (454 g) orecchiette

½ cup (120 ml) extra virgin olive oil, divided

10 cloves garlic, chopped

4 large jarred cherry peppers, chopped (seeds and stems removed), plus more for serving

Salt and pepper, to taste

¼ cup minced flat-leaf Italian parsley

Grated pecorino Romano cheese, for serving

INSTRUCTIONS

Bring a large pot of salted water to boil and blanch the broccoli rabe for 3 to 4 minutes, then place it on a plate and set aside to cool. Keep the water boiling.

In a large saucepan over medium-high heat, sauté the sausage until cooked through, about 10 minutes, breaking it up with a wooden spoon or meat masher. Remove the sausage from the pan and set it aside, leaving the fat in the pan.

Add the pasta to the same pot of boiling water used for the broccoli rabe and begin to cook to 1 to 2 minutes less than al dente.

While the pasta is cooking, combine ¼ cup of olive oil and the garlic in the same pan used for the sausage and cook over medium-low heat until the garlic turns golden, 1 to 2 minutes, stirring occasionally. Add the cherry peppers and return the sausage to the pan. Turn the heat back to medium and cook for 2 minutes more.

Add the broccoli rabe to the pan and mix everything together to combine. Drain the pasta, reserving 1½ cups (360 ml) of the pasta water. Add 1 cup of pasta water to the pan and cook for 1 minute more. Add in the almost-cooked pasta and cook until done, 1 to 2 minutes.

Taste-test and add salt and pepper as needed. When satisfied, turn off the heat and add in the parsley and the remaining ¼ cup of extra virgin olive oil. Mix once more, and if the pasta is too dry, add a little of the pasta water at a time to bring the consistency back to perfect. Serve with more cherry peppers and grated pecorino Romano cheese. Enjoy!

If you can't find bulk Italian sausage, buy sausage links, cut a slit down the middle, and remove the sausage from its casing.

Broccoli rabe is a bitter green and for many, an acquired taste. If you're not a fan of broccoli rabe, you can use spinach, escarole, or broccoli in its place.

Be sure to reserve your pasta water, as it is an essential part of this dish.

SIP & FEAST TIPS

CHICKEN RIGGIES

MAKES: 6–8 SERVINGS • PREP: 5 MINUTES • COOK: 40 MINUTES

Combining rigatoni and chicken with hot cherry and bell peppers in a creamy tomato-based pink sauce sounds like a fabulous idea, but it wasn't until we received multiple requests from our audience for "Chicken Riggies" that we knew this dish existed and that it had a name.

Chicken Riggies hails from Utica, New York, and is traditionally made with rigatoni, hence the "riggies." We're so grateful our audience shared this dish with us, and hope we've done you proud!

INGREDIENTS

- 2 pounds (908 g) boneless skinless chicken thighs
- Salt and pepper, to taste
- ¼ cup (60 ml) extra virgin olive oil, divided
- 2 large red bell peppers, sliced
- 8 cloves garlic, chopped
- 5 medium jarred cherry peppers, coarsely chopped (seeds and stems removed)
- 1 cup (240 ml) dry white wine
- 1 pound (454 g) rigatoni
- 1 (28-ounce) can crushed plum tomatoes
- 1 cup (240 ml) heavy cream
- ½ cup (45 g) grated pecorino Romano cheese
- ¼ cup packed basil leaves, hand torn

INSTRUCTIONS

Bring a large pot of salted water to boil.

Pat the chicken thighs dry and season with salt and pepper on both sides. Heat 2 tablespoons of the olive oil in a large pan over medium heat and sear the chicken until cooked through, 5 to 6 minutes per side, then move the chicken to a plate and cover with tented foil.

If the pan is dry, add the remaining 2 tablespoons of olive oil, and add the bell peppers to the pan. Sauté for 7 to 10 minutes or until they take on some color and soften. Add the garlic and cook for 2 minutes more or until it turns golden.

Add the cherry peppers and cook for 1 minute, then add the wine. Turn the heat to high and cook until the liquid reduces by half, 2 to 3 minutes. Using a wooden spoon, gently dislodge the brown bits from the bottom of the pan.

Add the pasta to the boiling water and cook to 1 minute less than al dente.

While the pasta is cooking, add the tomatoes to the sauce and bring it to a lively simmer for 5 minutes or so, then turn the heat to a touch less than medium. Add the cream and mix to incorporate. Slice the chicken into bite-sized pieces. Once the sauce starts to thicken, add the chicken and continue to simmer.

When the pasta is almost al dente, drain, reserving 2 cups (480 ml) of the pasta water. Add the pasta to the sauce and mix well to coat. If it's too thick, add ½ cup or more of reserved pasta water. Cook until the pasta reaches al dente, about 1 minute, then turn off the heat and remove the pan from the burner.

Add the pecorino and mix. Add a touch more pasta water if required to loosen up the sauce. Add the basil right before serving. Serve immediately.

If you'd like to increase the heat of the dish, add more cherry peppers. Conversely, if you prefer no heat, opt for sweet cherry peppers instead of the spicy ones.

Be sure to reserve your pasta water, as it is an essential part of this dish.

PAPPARDELLE WITH BRAISED SHORT RIB RAGU

MAKES: 6–8 SERVINGS • PREP: 20 MINUTES • COOK: 3 HOURS, 40 MINUTES

If it weren't for this recipe, I'm not sure you'd be reading this cookbook right now. For years this has been one of our most popular recipes, and the one that introduced so many of you to us, especially via YouTube. This recipe holds a special place in our hearts, and seemingly, the hearts of our readers.

And it's not hard to see why; hearty beef short ribs are braised in a fragrant tomato, herb, and red wine sauce until tender, then shredded and tossed with pappardelle and finished with plenty of Parmigiano-Reggiano. It's the perfect dish for cool nights when all you want to do is cozy up with a warm bowl of pasta and a glass of wine.

INGREDIENTS

- 10 (3-to-4-inch) bone-in short ribs, 3 to 4 pounds total (1.3 to 1.8 kg)
- 2 teaspoons kosher salt, plus more to taste
- ½ teaspoon ground black pepper, plus more to taste
- 1 tablespoon (15 ml) extra virgin olive oil
- 2 medium carrots, finely diced
- 1 medium onion, finely diced
- 2 cloves garlic, sliced
- ⅓ cup (85 g) tomato paste
- 2 cups (480 ml) dry red wine
- 1 (28-ounce) can plum tomatoes, hand crushed or pulsed in a blender
- 10 sprigs thyme
- 1 large bay leaf
- 1 pound (454 g) pappardelle
- ½ cup (45 g) grated Parmigiano-Reggiano cheese, for serving

INSTRUCTIONS

Preheat the oven to 300°F and set the rack to the middle level with enough room to accommodate a large Dutch oven and its lid.

Pat the short ribs dry and season with the salt and pepper on all sides. Heat a large Dutch oven over medium heat and once hot, add the olive oil. Add the short ribs to the pot, working in batches if needed to avoid crowding, and sear on all sides. The short ribs should take about 10 minutes per batch to sear on all sides.

Set the seared short ribs aside and turn the heat down to medium-low. Add the carrots, onion, and a pinch of salt and sauté in the beef fat until very soft, 10 to 15 minutes, then add the garlic and cook for 2 more minutes.

Add the tomato paste and cook for 3 minutes, stirring frequently. Add the wine and turn the heat to medium. Using a wooden spoon, gently dislodge the brown bits from the bottom of the pot.

Cook the wine for 3 minutes, then add the plum tomatoes, thyme, and bay leaf and bring to a simmer. Once simmering, add the short ribs to the pot, stir, then remove the pot from the heat and cover. Move the pot to the oven and cook for 2 hours. After 2 hours, partially uncover and continue to cook for 1 more hour.

Remove the pot from the oven, then remove the short ribs and place them on a large cutting board. Using two forks, shred the meat and discard any hard pieces of fat and the bones. Remove and discard the thyme stems and the bay leaf. Return the shredded meat to the pot and keep the ragu warm over low heat. Taste-test and season with salt and pepper to taste.

Bring a large pot of salted water to boil and cook the pappardelle until 1 minute less than al dente. Drain, reserving about 1 cup (240 ml) of the pasta water. Heat a large pan over a touch less than medium heat and add 2½ cups of the short rib ragu. Add the pasta to the pan and cook for 1 more minute, mixing well to thoroughly coat the pasta.

If the pasta needs more ragu, add more at this point. If the sauce seems a little dry, add a bit of reserved pasta water to loosen it up. Plate the pasta and top with the grated Parmigiano-Reggiano. Any remaining ragu and cheese can be served on the side.

Take the time to get a great sear on all sides of the short ribs. To do this, you'll likely need to work in batches. This will increase the flavor of the ragu tremendously.
For even more flavor, make the ragu a day before you plan to eat it. The flavor will intensify and refrigeration will encourage the fat to rise to the top overnight, allowing you to easily remove as much as you want prior to reheating.
Be sure to reserve your pasta water, as it is an essential part of this dish.
SIP & FEAST TIPS

BAKED ZITI

MAKES: 6–8 SERVINGS • **PREP:** 10 MINUTES • **COOK:** 1 HOUR, 15 MINUTES

If you grew up in the New York metropolitan area, it's likely you've eaten baked ziti a few times. Next to penne alla vodka, it's one of the most widely served pastas at catered events, and usually makes an appearance on holidays. It's a dish beloved by Italian Americans, and if you're a fan of *The Sopranos*, you'll know how difficult a decision it was for Bobby Bacala to eat Karen's last ziti.

Baked ziti is often made with a meat sauce, but this particular recipe is meatless. And while the dish calls for ziti pasta, know that you can easily use penne, rigatoni, or many other shapes in its place. In Sicily, anelletti al forno is a popular baked pasta dish made with tiny O-shaped pasta.

FOR THE SAUCE

¼ cup (60 ml) extra virgin olive oil

1 medium onion, finely diced

6 cloves garlic, minced

¼ cup (60 g) tomato paste

2 (28-ounce) cans plum tomatoes, hand crushed or pulsed in a blender

Salt and pepper, to taste

¼ cup packed basil leaves, roughly chopped

FOR THE BAKED ZITI

1 pound (454 g) ziti

1 pound (454 g) whole-milk ricotta cheese

1 pound (454 g) whole-milk block mozzarella cheese, two-thirds cubed and one-third shredded

½ cup (45 g) grated pecorino Romano cheese

FOR THE SAUCE

Heat the olive oil in a large pot over medium heat and add the onion and a pinch of salt. Cook the onion until very soft, about 10 minutes, stirring occasionally, then add the garlic and cook for 2 to 3 minutes more or until fragrant.

Add the tomato paste and cook for 5 minutes, stirring with a wooden spoon. Add a splash of water and/or lower the heat if the paste starts to burn. Add the plum tomatoes and bring the sauce to a simmer.

Cook the sauce for 15 minutes uncovered at a low simmer, stirring frequently to avoid any sticking. Taste the sauce and season with salt and pepper as needed.

Keep the sauce warm and set aside. Right before assembling the baked ziti, mix the basil into the sauce.

FOR THE BAKED ZITI

Preheat the oven to 375°F. Bring a large pot of salted water to boil and cook the pasta to 2 to 3 minutes less than al dente, per the package instructions.

In a large bowl, mix the cooked pasta with 3 cups of sauce and the ricotta cheese. Mix until smooth and creamy.

Coat a 9-x-13-inch baking dish with a thin layer of sauce. Add one-third of the sauced pasta. Sprinkle with half of the cubed mozzarella and one-third of the grated pecorino Romano and add a thin layer of sauce. Repeat for the next layer.

On the top layer add the remaining pasta, a bit more sauce, the shredded mozzarella, and the remaining pecorino Romano.

Bake for 25 to 30 minutes or until the cheese is bubbly and lightly browned. If a crispier top is desired, broil for 1 to 2 minutes, but watch carefully to avoid burning.

Remove from the oven and let the ziti sit for at least 10 minutes before serving with extra sauce on the side.

Take care to not overcook the ziti when boiling, since it will continue to cook in the oven for 30 minutes.

Add the pasta in layers with the cubes of mozzarella distributed randomly. This gives the dish a better texture where you get a bigger bite of cheese in one spot than another.

SIP & FEAST TIPS

STUFFED SHELLS

MAKES: 6–8 SERVINGS • **PREP:** 30 MINUTES • **COOK:** 45 MINUTES

When it comes to baked pasta, there are many options, but none appeal to my inner child the way stuffed shells do. I remember loving them for their shape as a kid, and being so excited any time I was lucky enough to have them, which most of the time was for a holiday, like Easter. They were definitely more of a special occasion–type pasta.

Now that I'm older, I find myself making them more frequently because they are actually very easy to make! Using a piping bag will make it easier to really pack the cheese into each shell, and using a quick red sauce, as opposed to a long-cooked meat sauce, cuts down on time.

This is definitely a dish that freezes well, so feel free to double the recipe, eat a batch now, and freeze the rest for a rainy day.

FOR THE SAUCE

- ¼ cup (60 ml) extra virgin olive oil
- 6 cloves garlic, sliced
- ½ teaspoon crushed hot red pepper flakes
- 3 tablespoons (45 g) tomato paste
- ½ cup (120 ml) water
- 3 (28-ounce) cans plum tomatoes, hand crushed or pulsed in a blender
- Salt and pepper, to taste
- 10 large basil leaves, hand torn

FOR THE SHELLS

- 1 pound (454 g) baby spinach
- 1 pound (454 g) jumbo shells (about 40 shells)
- 1½ pounds (680 g) whole-milk ricotta cheese, drained
- 3 cups (340 g) shredded whole-milk block mozzarella cheese, divided
- ¾ cup (68 g) grated pecorino Romano cheese, divided
- ½ cup minced flat-leaf Italian parsley
- ½ teaspoon garlic powder
- Salt and pepper, to taste
- 2 large eggs, beaten

FOR THE SAUCE

Heat the olive oil in a large pot or pan over medium heat and add the garlic. Sauté until golden, about 2 minutes, then add the red pepper flakes and cook for another 30 seconds.

Add the tomato paste and cook for 5 minutes, stirring frequently. If the paste starts to burn add some of the water. Add the remaining water and the plum tomatoes and bring the sauce to a lively simmer.

Taste and season with salt and pepper as needed. Turn the heat to low and partially cover the pot. Cook, making sure to stir occasionally, while you prepare the shells. Mix in the basil a few minutes before assembling the shells.

FOR THE SHELLS

Preheat the oven to 400°F and set the rack to the middle level.

Bring a large pot of salted water to boil and blanch the spinach for 30 seconds. Place the spinach in a fine-mesh strainer or a clean kitchen towel and squeeze out as much water as possible, then chop the spinach and set it aside.

Boil the shells in the same pot until very al dente, about 3 minutes less than package directions. Stir frequently to avoid sticking. Strain the shells and place them on clean kitchen towels to drain for a few minutes, then transfer to a parchment paper–lined baking sheet to avoid sticking. Allow the shells to cool before stuffing.

Combine the ricotta, 2 cups of the mozzarella, ½ cup of the pecorino, the chopped spinach, parsley, and garlic powder in a large bowl. Taste the ricotta mixture and season with salt and pepper. You want the stuffing to taste great! When satisfied with the taste, add the eggs and combine.

Ladle a thick layer of sauce (about 1 inch high) onto the bottom of one 13-x-18-inch or two 9-x-13-inch baking dishes.

To fill the shells, use either a small spoon or spatula or a pastry bag filled with the ricotta mixture. Spoon or pipe the filling into each shell. Place the filled shells into the baking dish, open side up.

Top the shells with more of the sauce but do not cover completely. Sprinkle the remaining 1 cup of mozzarella and ¼ cup of pecorino on top. Cover with a piece of parchment paper, then aluminum foil. Bake the shells for 20 minutes. After 20 minutes remove the covering and bake for 10 to 15 minutes more until bubbly and crisp. You can broil the top during the last 1 to 2 minutes, but watch carefully.

Let the shells sit for at least 10 minutes before serving with extra sauce on the side.

Spaghetti pie can be made with leftover spaghetti. If using leftover spaghetti that's already been sauced, you will not need to add all of the 3½ cups of sauce to the egg mixture.

The exact baking time will vary depending on your oven, but should be 12 to 15 minutes. Bake the spaghetti pie just until it sets before broiling to brown the top.

The pie can be flipped out of the pan and topped with more sauce, or it can be cut like a pie and served with sauce on the side.

RED SPAGHETTI PIE

MAKES: 8 SERVINGS • PREP: 5 MINUTES • COOK: 45 MINUTES

Spaghetti pie is a great way to get a second meal out of leftover pasta, and it is right in line with the "waste not, want not" dogma that so many Italian Americans live by. The eggs and cheese really extend the pasta, making it a bit of a cross between a frittata and a baked pasta.

While our recipe includes instructions for making a pound of pasta and adding it to the pie filling, you can easily use a leftover pound of cooked pasta if you've got it lying around. It will be better with leftover pasta!

A slice of spaghetti pie is great for dinner alongside a simple salad and a cup of soup, such as Italian Lentil Soup (page 168).

FOR THE SAUCE

- ⅓ cup (80 ml) extra virgin olive oil
- 1 medium onion, finely diced
- 8 cloves garlic, minced
- 3 tablespoons (45 g) tomato paste
- 2 (28-ounce) cans plum tomatoes, hand crushed or pulsed in a blender
- Salt and pepper, to taste

FOR THE PIE

- 1 pound (454 g) spaghetti
- 8 large eggs, beaten
- 2½ cups (280 g) diced block whole-milk mozzarella cheese
- ¾ cup (68 g) grated pecorino Romano cheese
- 3 tablespoons roughly chopped basil
- 1½ teaspoons cracked black pepper
- 1 teaspoon fine sea salt
- 3 tablespoons (45 ml) extra virgin olive oil

FOR THE SAUCE

Heat the olive oil in a large pan over medium heat. Add the onion and a pinch of salt and cook, stirring occasionally, until soft and translucent, about 7 minutes. Add the garlic and cook for 1 to 2 minutes. Once it turns golden and fragrant, add the tomato paste and cook for about 5 minutes, stirring frequently. Add a touch of water and/or lower the heat if the paste starts to burn.

Add the plum tomatoes and bring the sauce to a lively simmer for 5 minutes.

Reduce the heat to low and taste-test the sauce. Season with salt and pepper as needed.

FOR THE PIE

Preheat the oven to 375°F and set a rack on the middle level and another rack near the top.

Bring a large pot of salted water to boil and cook the spaghetti to 2 minutes less than al dente.

Meanwhile, in a large bowl, mix together the eggs, mozzarella, pecorino, basil, pepper, and salt. Add 3½ cups of the sauce and mix well.

Heat a 10-inch ovenproof pan, ideally cast iron, over medium heat.

Drain the spaghetti, add it to the egg and sauce mixture, and mix well to combine.

Add the oil to the hot pan and spread so it coats the whole pan. Add the spaghetti mixture to the pan and cook for 1 minute without stirring, then turn off the heat.

Bake for 12 to 15 minutes in the center of the oven or until the spaghetti pie is set. If a crispier top is desired, broil for 1 to 2 minutes, but watch carefully to avoid burning.

Let the spaghetti pie sit for 5 minutes, then cut into slices and serve with the remaining sauce.

BAKED PENNE WITH ITALIAN SAUSAGE

MAKES: 6–8 SERVINGS • **PREP:** 10 MINUTES • **COOK:** 1 HOUR

Baked penne with Italian sausage has everything you want in baked pasta. Creamy ricotta and mozzarella are tossed with penne and layered with an easy sausage tomato sauce, then baked until the mozzarella is melted and the penne is lightly crisp on the top. Perfect for those cooler nights when you just want to cozy up with a hearty baked pasta and a glass of wine!

I've used mild Italian sausage with fennel here, but you can easily use hot sausage. Both will add tremendous flavor, which really sets this one apart from other baked pastas that typically just use ground beef.

FOR THE SAUCE

¼ cup (60 ml) extra virgin olive oil

1 medium onion, diced

1½ pounds (680 g) bulk sweet or hot Italian sausage

4 cloves garlic, sliced

½ teaspoon crushed hot red pepper flakes, optional

½ cup (120 ml) dry white wine

2 (28-ounce) cans plum tomatoes, hand crushed or pulsed in a blender

Salt and pepper, to taste

FOR THE BAKED PENNE

1 pound (454 g) penne

1 pound (454 g) whole-milk ricotta cheese

1 pound (454 g) shredded whole-milk block mozzarella cheese, divided

½ cup (45 g) grated pecorino Romano cheese

FOR THE SAUCE

Heat the olive oil in a large pan or pot over medium heat and sauté the onion for 3 minutes. Add the sausage to the pan and turn the heat up to medium-high. Cook the sausage until browned, 7 to 10 minutes, making sure to break it up with a wooden spoon or meat masher. Add the garlic and cook for 2 to 3 more minutes or until fragrant. Add the red pepper flakes and cook for 30 seconds more.

Add the wine to the pan and turn the heat to high. Once the wine has mostly evaporated, turn the heat back down to medium and add the tomatoes. Bring to a simmer, stirring occasionally, then taste the sauce and season with salt and pepper as needed. Let the sauce simmer on low while you move to the next step.

FOR THE BAKED PENNE

Preheat the oven to 375°F and set the rack to the middle level.

While the sauce is simmering, bring a large pot of salted water to boil and cook the pasta to 2 minutes less than al dente.

Spread a ¼-inch-thick layer of sauce on the bottom of a 9-x-13-inch baking dish.

Place 4 cups of sauce into a large bowl and add the pasta. Add the ricotta, three-quarters of the mozzarella, and the pecorino. Mix well.

Pour the pasta into the baking dish. Top with a thin layer of sauce and the remaining mozzarella. Bake for 25 minutes or until browned on top. For extra color, broil for 1 to 2 more minutes, but watch carefully. Let the baked penne sit for at least 10 minutes before serving.

If you can't find bulk sausage, you can buy sausage links, cut a slit down the middle, and remove the sausage from its casing.

Ziti, rigatoni, or any tubular pasta can be used in place of penne.

Take care to not overcook the penne when boiling, since it will continue to cook in the oven for 25 minutes.

ORZO WITH LAMB RAGU

MAKES: 6–8 SERVINGS • **PREP:** 15 MINUTES • **COOK:** 2 HOURS, 45 MINUTES

This incredibly hearty and rich lamb ragu with orzo is a dish I've been making for years now, but I never actually wrote the recipe down until I decided to add it to this book.

The flavors in this dish are Greek-inspired and pair perfectly with the lamb, and it's an all-around great dish to make when the weather cools down. Crumbled block feta cheese makes an excellent addition at the end, rounding out the dish and adding to the Mediterranean flavor.

INGREDIENTS

¼ cup (60 ml) extra virgin olive oil

2 pounds (908 g) boneless lamb shoulder, trimmed of excess fat and cut into cubes

Salt and pepper, to taste

2 large onions, finely diced

3 tablespoons (45 g) tomato paste

1½ cups (360 ml) low-sodium beef stock

1 cup (240 ml) dry red wine

1 (28-ounce) can plum tomatoes, hand crushed or pulsed in a blender

1 teaspoon dried Greek oregano

1 cinnamon stick

2 large bay leaves

½ teaspoon ground nutmeg

1 pound (454 g) orzo

3 tablespoons minced flat-leaf Italian parsley

Feta cheese, for serving

INSTRUCTIONS

Preheat the oven to 300°F and set a rack to the middle to accommodate a large Dutch oven and its lid.

Heat the oil in a large Dutch oven over medium heat. Pat the lamb dry and season with salt and pepper on all sides, then add to the pot, working in batches to avoid overcrowding, and sear until browned on all sides, 5 to 7 minutes. Place the seared lamb on a plate and set aside.

Add the onions and a pinch of salt to the pot and sauté until very soft, 12 to 15 minutes.

Add the tomato paste and cook for 3 minutes, stirring frequently. Add a splash of water if the paste starts to burn. Add the beef stock and wine and bring to a boil while using a wooden spoon to gently dislodge any brown bits from the bottom of the pan.

Add the plum tomatoes, oregano, cinnamon stick, bay leaves, and nutmeg and bring to a simmer. Once simmering, add the lamb pieces to the pot and stir, then turn off the heat and cover the pot. Cook the lamb in the oven until tender, about 2 hours.

Remove the pot from the oven and place on a burner over low heat. Mix in the orzo and cover. Cook over low heat for 15 minutes, then check the orzo. If the pot is too dry, add a bit of water or beef stock.

Once the orzo is cooked remove the cinnamon stick and bay leaves and discard. Taste-test, adjusting the salt and pepper if necessary. Mix in the parsley and serve in bowls with crumbled feta on top.

Ground lamb can be used in place of the whole lamb shoulder. Ground lamb tends to have more fat than the shoulder, so feel free to remove some of the fat by spooning it out before adding the tomatoes.

Making the lamb ragu a day in advance and refrigerating it overnight will yield even better flavor. You can make the ragu, refrigerate, reheat, then add the orzo. Add extra beef stock or water if required.

The flavor of feta cheese complements this dish perfectly, but feel free to use parmesan or pecorino if you're not a fan of feta.

MANICOTTI

MAKES: 6 SERVINGS • **PREP:** 30 MINUTES • **COOK:** 1 HOUR

When making manicotti, you have two options. You can choose to buy manicotti pasta shells from the grocery store (I do this for the manicotti recipe on our website), or you can make homemade crepes. My hope is that by the time you're done reading this recipe, you'll choose the crepe option. They're nowhere near as difficult as you'd imagine, and each crepe cooks in about 2 minutes. But the best part is how light and airy the crepes are in juxtaposition to the heavy but delicious cheese and spinach filling.

FOR THE CREPES (CRESPELLE)

3 large eggs

1¼ cups (300 ml) whole milk

1 tablespoon (15 ml) extra virgin olive oil

1 cup (130 g) all-purpose flour

½ teaspoon fine sea salt

Cooking spray, butter, or oil, for the crepe pan

FOR THE SAUCE

¼ cup (60 ml) extra virgin olive oil, divided

1 pound (454 g) ground chuck

1 large onion, finely diced

1 medium carrot, finely diced

6 cloves garlic, sliced

½ teaspoon crushed hot red pepper flakes

3 tablespoons (45 g) tomato paste

3 (28-ounce) cans plum tomatoes, hand crushed or pulsed in a blender

½ cup (120 ml) water

Salt and pepper, to taste

10 large basil leaves, hand torn

FOR THE CREPES

Combine the eggs, milk, olive oil, flour, and salt in a blender and blend on high for 30 seconds, scraping down the sides as needed. Transfer the batter to a large bowl, cover with plastic wrap, and let it rest for 30 minutes. While the batter rests, you can skip ahead to prepare the sauce.

When the batter is ready, slowly heat a crepe pan or medium nonstick frying pan over slightly less than medium heat and add a touch of cooking spray, butter, or oil.

Once the pan is hot, pour enough batter to coat the pan and immediately swirl the batter in the pan by holding the handle and tilting the pan. Any excess batter can be poured back into the bowl.

Cook the crepe for about 1 minute on the first side. Once it starts curling at the edge of the pan and bubbles start to form, flip it with a spatula. Cook the other side for only 30 to 45 seconds, then place on a plate or baking sheet. Repeat the process and stack the subsequent cooked crepes on top of each other.

FOR THE SAUCE

Heat 2 tablespoons of the olive oil in a large pot or pan over a touch higher than medium heat and add the ground beef. Cook until browned, 7 to 10 minutes, breaking it up into small pieces with a wooden spoon or meat masher. Once well browned, remove the beef with a slotted spoon, place on a plate, and set aside.

Turn the heat down to medium and add the remaining 2 tablespoons of olive oil, the onion, carrot, and a pinch of salt. Sauté until very soft, 10 to 15 minutes, adding a splash of water and/or lowering the heat if the vegetables start to burn. Add the garlic and cook until fragrant, 2 to 3 minutes. Add the red pepper flakes and cook for another 30 seconds.

Add the tomato paste and cook for 5 minutes, stirring frequently. If the paste starts to burn, add a splash of water. Return the browned beef to the pot, add the plum tomatoes and water, and bring the sauce to a lively simmer.

Taste-test and season with salt and pepper as needed. Turn the heat to low, cover the pot with the lid cracked, and cook while you prepare the crepes, making sure to stir occasionally to prevent sticking. Mix in the basil a few minutes before assembling the manicotti.

CONTINUED

MANICOTTI (CONTINUED)

FOR THE FILLING

1 pound (454 g) whole-milk ricotta cheese, drained

2 cups (227 g) shredded whole-milk block mozzarella cheese

½ cup (45 g) grated pecorino Romano cheese, plus more for serving

½ pound (226 g) chopped frozen spinach, thawed and squeezed dry

¼ cup minced flat-leaf Italian parsley

Salt and pepper, to taste

1 large egg, beaten

FOR THE MANICOTTI

Preheat the oven to 350°F.

Combine the ricotta, mozzarella, pecorino, spinach, and parsley in a large bowl. Taste-test the ricotta mixture and season with salt and pepper if required. When satisfied with the taste, add the beaten egg and combine.

Ladle a thick layer of sauce (about 1 inch) into the bottom of one 13-x-18-inch or two 9-x-13-inch baking dishes.

Lay out a crepe and add 3 to 4 tablespoons of the ricotta mixture on the lower third of the crepe, then roll tightly into a cigar shape. Place the manicotti into the baking dish seam side down. Repeat with all the remaining crepes and filling.

Top the manicotti with more of the sauce, but do not cover completely. Cover with a piece of parchment paper, then aluminum foil. Bake for 20 minutes, then remove the covering and bake for an additional 10 to 15 minutes or until bubbly and crisp.

Let the manicotti sit for at least 10 minutes before serving with extra sauce and grated cheese on the side.

Crepes cook very quickly, which means they can burn easily. If one starts to burn, simply remove the pan from the burner, lower the heat a touch, and resume after a few minutes. It is highly recommended that you use a crepe pan or flat griddle pan for best results.

The crepe batter will yield 12 to 16 eight-inch crepes, depending on how thickly the batter was poured.

For a meatless version you can either omit the ground beef, or use our marinara sauce recipe (see page 57).

RISO AL FORNO

MAKES: 6–8 SERVINGS • **PREP:** 10 MINUTES • **COOK:** 1 HOUR, 30 MINUTES

There are few things more comforting than baked pastas, but baked rice, or riso al forno, is up there! This dish is an homage to Sicilian flavors with the addition of peas and scamorza cheese, but I encourage you to use this recipe as a jumping-off point and add any other ingredients you'd like.

My grandma would make this often, and each time a little differently; sometimes she'd include roasted eggplant instead of the meat, especially on Fridays in Lent. No matter how she'd make it, I always loved it just as much as I did pasta al forno.

Because riso al forno is made with rice and is naturally gluten-free, it is a wonderful alternative for those who can't have regular pasta. We like to serve this as a main course alongside a simple sautéed green, but it can also be served as a pasta course before the main course.

FOR THE SAUCE

- 2 tablespoons (30 ml) extra virgin olive oil
- 2 pounds (908 g) ground chuck
- 1 medium onion, diced
- 5 cloves garlic, sliced
- 2 anchovy fillets, optional
- ½ teaspoon crushed hot red pepper flakes, optional
- ⅓ cup (85 g) tomato paste
- 2 (28-ounce) cans plum tomatoes, hand crushed or pulsed in a blender
- Salt and pepper, to taste

FOR THE RISO AL FORNO

- 2½ cups (500 g) arborio rice
- 2 cups (340 g) frozen peas, thawed
- 2 cups (226 g) shredded scamorza cheese
- ¾ cup (68 g) grated pecorino Romano cheese
- ¼ cup packed basil leaves, roughly chopped

FOR THE SAUCE

Heat the olive oil in a large saucepan over medium-high heat. Add the beef and cook, stirring occasionally, until browned, 7 to 10 minutes. Remove the meat and place on a plate, leaving 3 to 4 tablespoons of fat in the pan.

Turn the heat down to medium and add the onion along with a pinch of salt. Sauté until soft, 5 to 7 minutes, then add the garlic and anchovies and cook for 2 to 3 minutes more or until fragrant and the anchovies dissolve. Add the red pepper flakes, if using, and cook for another 30 seconds.

Return the meat to the pan and add the tomato paste. Cook for 5 minutes, stirring frequently.

Add the plum tomatoes and mix in to incorporate. Once the sauce starts bubbling, turn the heat down to a very low simmer and cook for at least 20 minutes, uncovered, stirring occasionally to avoid any sticking. Taste-test the sauce and adjust the salt and pepper as needed.

FOR THE RISO AL FORNO

Preheat the oven to 375°F and set the rack to the middle level.

While the sauce is simmering, parboil the rice in salted water for 8 minutes. Drain the rice and rinse under cold water, then mix with the peas.

Set aside 3 cups of the sauce for later. In a very large bowl, combine the rice and peas with the remaining sauce. Mix in half of the scamorza cheese, half of the pecorino, and the basil.

Coat a 9-x-13-inch baking dish with 1½ cups of the reserved sauce. Pour the rice mixture into the dish and top with the remaining sauce and cheese.

Bake the rice for 30 to 35 minutes or until tender. For extra color, broil for 1 to 2 minutes, but watch carefully to avoid burning. Allow the riso al forno to settle for at least 15 minutes before serving.

Scamorza cheese can be hard to find, depending on where you live. Feel free to use smoked or regular mozzarella cheese in its place.

Be sure to only partially cook (parboil) the rice on the stovetop, since it will continue to cook and become tender in the oven.

To make a vegetarian version, use marinara sauce (see page 57) in place of the meat sauce.

CREAMY POLENTA

MAKES: 4 SERVINGS • PREP: 5 MINUTES • COOK: 1 HOUR

As a kid, polenta was never a thing in my home. In fact, I didn't even know what it was until I started watching the Food Network as a teenager. I'm pretty sure my experience with polenta, or lack thereof, is similar to that of many kids growing up in Italian American households on Long Island. For the most part, our ancestors came from southern Italy, whereas polenta is a thing of the north.

Nevertheless, I'm glad I discovered polenta because it is truly the perfect base or side to so many wonderful dishes, such as Peposo (page 175). While it takes about an hour to make, it really is quite simple, so don't be intimidated!

INGREDIENTS

5 cups (1.2 L) water

1 cup (160 g) polenta

1 cup (90 g) grated Parmigiano-Reggiano cheese, plus more to taste

4 tablespoons (56 g) butter, plus more to taste

Salt, to taste

INSTRUCTIONS

Bring the water to boil in a deep pot or Dutch oven. Once boiling, whisk in the polenta and stir frequently. Once the polenta starts splattering, lower the heat to medium-low and cover, leaving the lid partially cracked open.

Continue to cook at moderate to low heat, stirring every so often while wiping down the sides of the pot with a spoon, until the polenta is completely smooth and no longer gritty (50 to 60 minutes). If the polenta becomes too thick, add more water about ½ cup at a time and stir until creamy.

Remove the pot from the heat and mix in the cheese and butter. Season with salt and more cheese and butter to taste, and serve.

I highly recommend using a cover to help prevent the polenta from splattering while it cooks. It also minimizes the need to constantly stir the polenta, although the polenta should be stirred frequently and the sides of the pot should be scraped down to dislodge any stuck polenta.

Follow a 5:1 ratio to scale this recipe: 5 parts water to 1 part polenta.

All milk in place of the water or half water/half milk makes an even creamier polenta.

SIP & FEAST TIPS

PERFECT RISOTTO MILANESE

MAKES: 6 SERVINGS • **PREP:** 10 MINUTES • **COOK:** 35 MINUTES

With its distinct yellow color and wonderfully creamy texture, risotto Milanese is a dish that everyone should experience at least once in their lives. For many, the thought of making risotto is intimidating, but I assure you that it's easier to make than you'd think, and my instructions aim to remove any guesswork!

Risotto Milanese is wonderful on its own as a pasta course, or can be served alongside meat, chicken, or fish. It's often served with a hearty dish like veal osso buco.

INGREDIENTS

8 cups (1.9 L) low-sodium beef stock, or chicken or vegetable stock

8 tablespoons (113 g) butter, divided

1 large shallot, finely diced

2 cups (400 g) arborio rice, or carnaroli or Vialone Nano

¾ cup (180 ml) dry white wine

½ teaspoon saffron threads

½ cup (120 ml) low-sodium beef stock, or chicken or vegetable stock, warm

1 cup (90 g) grated Parmigiano-Reggiano cheese, plus more for serving

3 tablespoons minced flat-leaf Italian parsley

Salt and pepper, to taste

INSTRUCTIONS

In a large saucepan, bring the beef stock to a low simmer.

Heat 3 tablespoons of the butter in a large nonstick pan over medium heat. Add the shallot and sauté until soft, 3 to 4 minutes.

Add the rice and stir frequently while continuing to cook for another 2 to 3 minutes, or until the rice turns a bit translucent at the edges.

Add the wine to the pan, turn the heat to high, and cook until the wine reduces by half, 2 to 3 minutes, then turn the heat down to a low simmer.

Add ½ cup of the simmering stock and cook, stirring occasionally. As the liquid evaporates, add another ½ cup of stock. Repeat the process until the risotto is al dente and creamy, but not overcooked, approximately 20 minutes. (You may not need to use all of the stock.)

Approximately 5 minutes before the risotto has finished, combine the saffron and the ½ cup of warm beef stock in a small bowl and set aside.

When satisfied with the consistency of the risotto, remove the pan from the heat and add the saffron mixture. Mix well, then add the remaining 5 tablespoons of butter, the cheese, and parsley. Taste-test and season well with salt and pepper as needed. Serve immediately.

For the best results, set up a cooking station ahead of time. Since risotto is a hands-on dish, having the proper setup will yield superior results. Prep your ingredients and place your stock pot close to your risotto pan so ladling the stock is easy.

While carnaroli rice is considered the "caviar" of risotto rice, arborio rice is more readily available and will work just as well!

The time in which risotto cooks may vary depending on your heat level. The best way to tell if risotto is done is to taste it. The consistency should be unbroken rice kernels that are al dente but creamy.

SIP & FEAST TIPS

THE ITALIAN AMERICAN SUNDAY DINNER

Sunday dinner was the meal I enjoyed most as a child and looked forward to all week long. Every Sunday my grandmother would wake at the crack of dawn to start preparing for it. She started her sauce (she called it gravy) early and allowed it to simmer all day. It included pork and beef meatballs, beef braciole, Italian sausages (hot and sweet), and pork chops. She always made a lot of it. Like a ton.

I can still remember waking up on Sunday mornings to the smell of her sauce. There was nothing like it. It took a lot of willpower not to sneak a taste every hour or so! Thankfully, I wouldn't have to wait too long, as we'd usually start eating dinner around 2 or 3 p.m. We'd gather around and wait anxiously while she brought her sauce to the table. There would always be some type of pasta to have with the sauce and the meat, vegetables, and of course a large dinner salad.

Grated cheese, usually pecorino Romano, but sometimes parmesan, would always be on the table, along with a few loaves of seeded Italian bread from the local bakery.

The next day I'd go to the bus stop and trade Sunday dinner stories with my friends, and argue passionately over whose mom or grandma made the best sauce.

The Sunday dinner tradition is alive and well today in many homes, and now that I'm an adult I have begun to realize it was about so much more than the food. It was knowing unequivocally that no matter what was going on in the outside world, or even within our own close circle, there would always be Sunday dinner. It was a constant, a comfort, and something to count on.

When Tara and I prepare Sunday dinner for our family, we always feel a sense of nostalgia. The smells, tastes, and feelings of well-being are rooted deep and ensure that those who came before us have an everlasting "seat" at our table.

THE ULTIMATE SUNDAY MENU

ANTIPASTO PLATTER—scale up or down depending on how many you're serving (see page 52)

RIGATONI WITH SUNDAY SAUCE AND MEATBALLS (page 58) and **BRACIOLE** (page 134)

ITALIAN CHICKEN CUTLETS (page 118) or **ITALIAN BAKED CHICKEN AND POTATOES** (page 113)

COLD BROCCOLI SALAD (page 204)

THE SUNDAY DINNER SALAD (page 191)

1 to 2 loaves of Italian bread with butter and olive oil on the side

Grated Parmigiano-Reggiano and pecorino Romano cheese, for topping the pasta

Italian cookies, such as **REGINA** (page 222), **PIGNOLI** (page 225), and **LEMON RICOTTA** (page 226)

ITALIAN CHEESECAKE (page 213)

CHOCOLATE CHIP RICOTTA CAKE (page 214)

Espresso, coffee, or tea

MAIN COURSES

It was quite the task to narrow down the main courses to include in this, our first cookbook. What Tara and I did here was include the very best of our main courses from our website—the ones with the highest ratings that our readers love, like Shrimp Oreganata (page 142) and Italian Baked Chicken and Potatoes (page 113)—and we added a few new ones as well. Through the years we've had many readers ask us for our Stuffed Calamari recipe (page 157), or for a recipe for New York–Style Eggplant Parm (page 154), and while those aren't on our website at this moment, we are happy to finally share those recipes with you here in this book.

As you look through the chapter, you'll see the main ingredients run the gamut, from chicken, beef, and pork to shrimp, salmon, and calamari. We hope you find main course recipes here that you'll love and make for years to come!

ITALIAN BAKED CHICKEN AND POTATOES

MAKES: 6 SERVINGS • **PREP:** 20 MINUTES • **COOK:** 50 MINUTES

Nothing says "welcome home" better than the smell of chicken and potatoes roasting, especially when there is oregano involved. There's something about it that is so comforting.

This is a dish I make very often for my family and one that is extremely popular among our readers. In fact, many have told us they had fond memories of eating chicken like this, but the person in their family who used to make it passed on without sharing the recipe, leaving it a mystery—until now.

If you're looking for a rustic, no-frills chicken and potatoes that tastes like nostalgia, look no further. This one is best served with some simple sautéed greens or a salad. In fact, The Sunday Dinner Salad (page 191) is the one we most often pair with our chicken and potatoes, and the combination is a home run.

INGREDIENTS

- 1 whole young chicken, cut into pieces and dried very well
- 6 medium potatoes, cut into 1-inch cubes
- 1 medium onion, diced
- 6 cloves garlic, minced
- ½ cup minced flat-leaf Italian parsley
- ½ cup (45 g) grated Parmigiano-Reggiano cheese
- 2 teaspoons dried oregano
- ¾ cup (180 ml) extra virgin olive oil, divided
- 2 teaspoons kosher salt, divided, plus more to taste
- 1 teaspoon ground black pepper, plus more to taste

INSTRUCTIONS

Preheat the oven to 375°F and set the rack to the middle level. Dry the chicken pieces and potatoes well with paper towels.

In a large bowl combine the onion, garlic, parsley, cheese, oregano, and ½ cup of the olive oil. Mix well. Dry the chicken off one more time, then season both sides with 1 teaspoon of the salt and the pepper. Add the chicken to the bowl and use your hands to really get the chicken coated!

Place the chicken in a single layer in a large baking dish, skin side up. Toss the potatoes into the bowl with the remaining olive oil mixture and mix well. Season the potatoes with a bit more salt and pepper, then place the potatoes around the chicken. If you cannot fit it all in the same dish, use another baking dish for the remaining potatoes.

Drizzle the remaining ¼ cup of olive oil onto the chicken and potatoes. Bake for 45 minutes. At the halfway point, spoon some of the juices on top of each piece of chicken and resume baking.

After 45 minutes the chicken should be almost cooked. If desired, you can broil the chicken for a few minutes to crisp up the skin, but watch carefully! The chicken is done when the internal temperature reaches 160 to 165°F.

Right when the chicken comes out, sprinkle it with the remaining 1 teaspoon of salt. Let the chicken sit lightly covered with tented foil for 10 to 15 minutes before serving. The chicken will reabsorb some of the pan juices and become moister. Right before serving toss the chicken and potatoes in the pan juices and serve.

If you noticed that I mention drying the chicken multiple times in this recipe, it's because it is that important. Chicken has a lot of water and that water needs to be removed to successfully roast. Wet chicken will steam, rather than roast, which can yield a rubbery texture.

It may seem like there's a lot of olive oil here, but it is necessary to ensure the chicken stays moist.

Use a digital instant-read thermometer to ensure the chicken reaches the proper temperature.

SIP & FEAST TIPS

CHICKEN SCARPARIELLO

MAKES: 8 SERVINGS • PREP: 15 MINUTES • COOK: 1 HOUR, 15 MINUTES

If you dine at any family-style Italian American restaurant in the New York metropolitan area, you'll likely find chicken scarpariello on the menu. It typically combines chicken, sausage, peppers, and garlic with a vinegar-based sauce and, depending on the restaurant, you may also find pearl onions, olives, or mushrooms.

While the Italian word *scarpariello* translates to "shoemaker-style" in English, I've learned after asking many restaurant staff that the dish means "chicken with a bunch of stuff." I share this with you to encourage you to make chicken scarp your own. Use our recipe as a base, but don't be afraid to add in some of your favorites. Peppadew peppers, roasted garlic, and cremini mushrooms would all be excellent here!

INGREDIENTS

- 2 pounds (908 g) small potatoes, halved
- ½ cup (120 ml) extra virgin olive oil, divided
- 1 tablespoon (10 g) kosher salt, divided
- 1 teaspoon ground black pepper, divided
- 1½ pounds (680 g) mild Italian sausage with fennel
- 2 large red bell peppers, sliced into ¼-inch strips
- 3 pounds (1.4 kg) bone-in chicken thighs, trimmed of overhanging fat
- 15 cloves garlic, halved
- 5 large jarred cherry peppers, quartered (seeds and stems removed)
- 1¼ cups (300 ml) dry white wine
- ¾ cup (180 ml) red wine vinegar
- 1¼ cups (300 ml) no-sodium chicken stock
- ½ cup minced flat-leaf Italian parsley

INSTRUCTIONS

Preheat the oven to 425°F and set the rack to the middle level. Line a baking sheet with parchment paper and set aside. In a large bowl, toss the potatoes with 6 tablespoons of the olive oil and season with ½ tablespoon of the salt and ½ teaspoon of the black pepper. Spread the potatoes on the parchment-lined baking sheet, cut side down. Roast the potatoes for 30 minutes or until nicely browned on the bottom sides.

Meanwhile, heat the remaining 2 tablespoons of olive oil in a large ovenproof frying pan over medium heat (a 14-inch pan works well). Add the sausage links and sear them on all sides until brown but not cooked all the way through, 7 to 10 minutes total. Remove the sausage links and set aside. When the links are cool enough to handle, slice them diagonally into bite-sized pieces.

Add the bell peppers to the same pan and cook, stirring occasionally, for a few minutes until they begin to soften. Remove the peppers to the same plate with the sausage, set aside, and cover with tented foil to keep warm.

Dry the chicken thighs very well with paper towels and season with the remaining ½ tablespoon salt and ½ teaspoon black pepper on all sides. Using the same pan and working in batches to avoid overcrowding, sear the chicken pieces skin side down until golden and crisp, then flip and cook for another 3 to 4 minutes. If required, use a bit more olive oil for searing. Place the seared chicken pieces on a plate and cover with tented foil to stay warm.

If there is too much oil and fat in the pan, remove some, leaving ¼ cup worth. Add the garlic and sauté until golden, then add the cherry peppers and cook for 2 minutes.

Add the wine and vinegar and turn the heat to high. Boil for 5 to 7 minutes or until the liquid reduces by half. Gently scrape the pan with a wooden spoon to dislodge any brown bits.

Add the chicken stock and bring to a boil once more. Reduce the liquid by half, about 5 minutes, then turn off the heat.

Add the bell peppers, sausage, and potatoes back to the pan and toss to coat with the sauce. Nestle the chicken pieces into the pan with the skin side facing up. Spoon the sauce on top of everything, then cover the pan tightly with foil. Bake in the oven for 20 minutes, then remove the foil and continue to bake for another 15 to 20 minutes or until the chicken reaches an internal temperature of 185 to 195°F.

When the chicken has finished cooking, add the parsley, toss to coat, and serve immediately.

Chicken thighs, and dark meat in general, are far more forgiving to cook with. They're also juicier, tend not to dry out, and are better cooked to at least 185°F internal temperature. While you can use chicken breasts for this recipe, I highly recommend using chicken thighs.

I love the flavor of Italian fennel sausage, but you can use sausage without fennel or even spicy sausage.

If you don't have an ovenproof 14-inch pan, the dish can be transferred to a large baking pan for roasting.

If you find the vinegar sauce to be a little thin, you can strain it and cook in a pan to further reduce.

This recipe calls for a whole chicken, but you can use bone-in or boneless chicken thighs (about 4 pounds worth if using bone-in). Be sure to dry the chicken pieces very well so they successfully roast. If using just chicken thighs, cook them to an internal temperature of 185 to 195°F.

Artichoke hearts make a great addition to this dish and pair well with all the flavors. You can also add lemon slices to the sauce at the very end.

Use a digital instant-read thermometer to ensure the chicken reaches the proper temperature.

CHICKEN VESUVIO

MAKES: 6–8 SERVINGS • PREP: 10 MINUTES • COOK: 1 HOUR, 10 MINUTES

Hailing from the windy city of Chicago, this one-pan Italian American dish consists of chicken pieces nestled beside potato wedges and roasted until golden in a lemon-garlic white wine sauce. Green peas are added at the end for flavor, texture, and a bit of brightness. The result is one of the best family-style chicken dishes you'll ever have.

Because chicken Vesuvio is a one-pan dish, you don't need to serve anything else with it, although a salad or sautéed greens wouldn't hurt.

INGREDIENTS

- 4 to 5 medium Yukon Gold potatoes, cut into wedges
- ½ cup (120 ml) extra virgin olive oil, divided
- 2 teaspoons dried oregano, divided, plus more to taste
- 2 teaspoons kosher salt, divided, plus more to taste
- 1 teaspoon ground black pepper, divided, plus more to taste
- 1 whole young chicken, cut into pieces and dried very well
- 10 cloves garlic, roughly chopped
- 1 cup (240 ml) dry white wine
- 1 cup (240 ml) low-sodium chicken stock
- 2 tablespoons (30 ml) fresh lemon juice, plus more to taste
- 2 cups (340 g) frozen peas, thawed
- 4 tablespoons (56 g) butter, cubed
- 3 tablespoons minced flat-leaf Italian parsley

INSTRUCTIONS

Preheat the oven to 450°F and set one rack to the lowest level and the other to the middle level. Line a baking sheet with parchment paper and set aside.

Toss the potatoes in a large bowl with ¼ cup of the olive oil, 1 teaspoon of the oregano, 1 teaspoon of the salt, and ½ teaspoon of the pepper. Spread the potatoes onto the parchment-lined baking sheet and roast on the lowest oven rack for 20 minutes or until well browned on one side. After removing the potatoes, turn the oven down to 375°F.

Heat a large stainless steel frying pan over medium heat. Pat the chicken pieces very dry and season with the remaining 1 teaspoon of oregano, 1 teaspoon of salt, and ½ teaspoon of pepper.

Add a touch of olive oil to the pan. Working in batches to avoid overcrowding the pan, sear the chicken skin side down for 5 minutes, then 3 to 4 minutes on the other side. Remove the chicken and place in a large roasting pan skin side up.

If the frying pan is dry, add 1 to 2 tablespoons more olive oil. Add the garlic and sauté until golden.

Add the wine and chicken stock and turn the heat to high. Cook for 4 to 5 minutes to let the sauce reduce by about half. During the last minute, add the lemon juice, then turn the heat off.

Pour the sauce around the chicken, then nestle the roasted potatoes around the chicken pieces. Bake on the middle rack for 25 to 30 minutes or until the chicken reaches an internal temperature of 160°F. If desired, broil for the last 2 minutes for more color on top, but watch carefully to avoid burning.

To finish the dish, transfer the chicken and potatoes to a platter and cover with tented foil. Transfer the sauce to a large saucepan and cook over medium heat. Add the peas to the sauce and bring to a simmer, then once the peas are hot, turn off the heat and whisk in the butter one cube at a time. Season to taste with more salt, pepper, oregano, and lemon juice if needed, then pour the sauce on top of the chicken and potatoes. Top with the parsley and serve immediately.

ITALIAN CHICKEN CUTLETS

MAKES: 4 SERVINGS • **PREP:** 20 MINUTES • **COOK:** 20 MINUTES

There's nothing like a plate of Italian chicken cutlets! They truly are a busy person's best friend because they can be used for so many other dishes, but they're also wonderful on their own with a squeeze of lemon.

I find myself making big batches (four to five times this recipe!) of these when the kids go back to school because they're versatile enough to send on sandwiches for lunch, but also make a great weeknight dinner along with some rice pilaf and sautéed greens, topped with tomatoes and fresh mozzarella, or atop a simple arugula salad with lemon and shaved Parmigiano-Reggiano.

One of the best ways to use these cutlets is to top them with marinara sauce (see page 57) and shredded mozzarella, bake at 450°F for 5 to 7 minutes, and sprinkle with parmesan. You've got chicken parm!

INGREDIENTS

- ½ cup (65 g) all-purpose flour, for dredging
- 1½ teaspoons kosher salt, divided
- ½ teaspoon ground black pepper, divided
- 3 large eggs
- 1 cup (100 g) Italian seasoned breadcrumbs
- ¼ cup (23 g) grated pecorino Romano cheese
- 3 tablespoons minced flat-leaf Italian parsley
- 1 pound (454 g) thin-sliced chicken cutlets
- Olive oil or neutral oil, for frying
- 1 large lemon, cut into wedges, for serving

INSTRUCTIONS

In a large bowl, combine the flour with ¾ teaspoon of the salt and ¼ teaspoon of the pepper. In another large bowl beat the eggs. Finally, in a third large bowl, combine the breadcrumbs, pecorino, parsley, and the remaining ¾ teaspoon salt and ¼ teaspoon pepper. Line a baking sheet with parchment paper and set aside.

Pat the chicken dry, then dredge in the flour. Shake off the excess, and place into the egg wash. Make sure the egg completely coats the flour, then lift each cutlet out of the bowl, allowing the excess egg to drip off. Place the chicken into the breadcrumbs. Coat on both sides and set the breaded chicken cutlets onto the parchment-lined baking sheet.

Pour enough oil into a large cast iron or heavy pan to fill it at least 1 inch high, and heat until the temperature reaches 360°F.

Working in batches to avoid crowding the pan, fry the cutlets for 3 to 4 minutes per side. When the cutlets finish cooking, set them on a wire rack or a plate lined with paper towels.

Serve the cutlets with the lemon wedges.

If you need a touch more breadcrumbs, flour, or egg, just add as needed. The thickness of the cutlets will determine how much of these ingredients are necessary.

Fillet the chicken and pound each piece to no more than ½ inch thick. The thinner the cutlets, the better they'll be.

Use an oil thermometer to take the guesswork out of frying.

SIP & FEAST TIPS

Thinly sliced chicken breasts will yield superior results and are the universal choice for chicken Francese.
It is recommended to use a nonstick pan to prevent the egg from sticking.
Regulating your heat is very important since the butter can burn easily.
SIP & FEAST TIPS

CHICKEN FRANCESE

MAKES: 4–6 SERVINGS • PREP: 20 MINUTES • COOK: 25 MINUTES

Growing up on Long Island, chicken Francese was as common a dish as any; in fact, it was one of the first dishes I learned how to cook!

Sometimes spelled chicken Francaise, or referred to as "chicken French," it's available in nearly every Italian American restaurant in the New York metropolitan area, and I believe that's because its buttery lemon flavor appeals to the masses.

Chicken Francese is great alongside rice pilaf and a green vegetable, such as sautéed broccoli rabe, or a bed of garlicky spinach; a chunk of crusty bread is great too! It also makes an excellent sandwich when placed on toasted garlic bread and topped with melted mozzarella.

INGREDIENTS

4 large eggs

¼ cup minced flat-leaf Italian parsley, divided

Salt and pepper, to taste

½ cup (65 g) all-purpose flour, for dredging

4 tablespoons (56 g) butter, cubed and divided

4 tablespoons (60 ml) olive oil, divided, as needed

1½ pounds (680 g) thin-sliced chicken cutlets

1 large shallot, minced

1½ cups (360 ml) low-sodium chicken stock

½ cup (120 ml) dry white wine

1 large lemon, sliced

2 tablespoons (30 ml) fresh lemon juice, plus more to taste

INSTRUCTIONS

First, set up a frying station. In a large bowl, beat the eggs together and mix in 2 tablespoons of the minced parsley and a pinch of salt and pepper. Mix the flour with a pinch of salt and pepper in a large bowl or on a plate for easier dredging.

Heat 2 tablespoons of the butter and 1 tablespoon of the olive oil in a large nonstick pan over medium heat.

Quickly season the chicken cutlets with salt and pepper on both sides. Dredge the chicken in the flour, then shake off the excess and dip into the egg and parsley mixture. Gently place the cutlets into the pan, working in batches to avoid crowding the pan. Fry for 3 to 4 minutes per side or until golden brown. Transfer the chicken from the pan to a plate and cover with tented foil to keep warm. Use more oil as required for the next batch. Reserve the leftover flour mixture and set aside.

Add the shallot and a pinch of salt to the same pan and sauté until soft and translucent, 2 to 3 minutes.

Add the chicken stock and wine, turn the heat to high, and bring the sauce to a boil while gently scraping the bottom of the pan with a wooden spoon to dislodge any brown bits. Boil for about 5 minutes or until it reduces by about half and starts to thicken.

Turn the heat to slightly less than medium and add the lemon slices. Roll the remaining 2 tablespoons of butter in the leftover flour mixture and add them to the sauce one at a time, whisking to combine. Cook for 2 to 3 minutes or until the sauce thickens.

Mix in the lemon juice, taste the sauce, and adjust the salt and pepper to taste. Also, if needed, add more lemon juice to taste.

When satisfied with the taste, return the chicken to the pan and gently coat with the sauce and heat through for 2 to 3 minutes. Sprinkle the remaining 2 tablespoons of parsley on top and remove the pan from the heat. Serve immediately.

SPINACH MUSHROOM CHICKEN

MAKES: 4–6 SERVINGS • **PREP:** 10 MINUTES • **COOK:** 30 MINUTES

On busy weeknights we try our best to make healthy-ish dishes that can be made quickly and with just a few ingredients, and this one checks all the boxes. Since the chicken cutlets are pounded thin, they can be cooked in under 10 minutes, and ditto for the mushrooms and the white wine garlic sauce. The whole dish comes together in no time, and because it's made in one pan, it's easier to clean up.

This one is great served over rice or alongside roasted potatoes, but truth be told, our favorite way to eat it is with a loaf of crusty bread to mop up the delicious sauce.

INGREDIENTS

- 2 pounds (908 g) thin-sliced chicken cutlets
- Salt and pepper, for seasoning, plus more to taste
- ½ cup (65 g) all-purpose flour, for dredging
- ¼ cup (60 ml) extra virgin olive oil, as needed
- 1 pound (454 g) cremini mushrooms, sliced
- 5 cloves garlic, sliced
- 1 cup (240 ml) low-sodium chicken stock
- ¾ cup (180 ml) dry white wine
- ¾ pound (340 g) baby spinach
- 3 tablespoons (42 g) butter

FOR THE CORNSTARCH SLURRY (OPTIONAL)

- 2 tablespoons (15 g) cornstarch
- ¼ cup (60 ml) water

INSTRUCTIONS

Cut the chicken into roughly 3-inch-long pieces, pat dry with paper towels, and season well with salt and pepper on both sides. Dredge the chicken in flour on all sides and shake off the excess.

Heat 1 to 2 tablespoons of the oil in a large skillet over medium heat. Once hot, add the chicken pieces, working in batches to avoid overcrowding the pan. Sear the chicken for 3 minutes per side or until cooked through, then place on a plate and lightly cover with tented foil. Add more oil as needed as you cook the remaining batches.

Add the mushrooms to the pan and cook, stirring occasionally, until browned, 5 to 7 minutes. Once browned add the garlic to the pan and cook for 2 minutes more.

Season the mushrooms with salt and pepper to taste, then add the chicken stock and wine to the pan and turn the heat to high. With a wooden spoon, gently scrape the bottom of the pan to dislodge any brown bits. Cook until the liquid reduces by half, 3 to 5 minutes, then turn the heat down to medium.

Add the chicken and the spinach to the pan, cover, and cook for 2 to 3 minutes to wilt the spinach and warm the chicken through.

If the sauce is too loose, stir the cornstarch and water together to make the optional cornstarch slurry. Add half the slurry to the pan and cook over medium-high heat until thickened, about 2 minutes. If it's still too loose, add the remaining slurry. When satisfied with the consistency, turn the heat off and remove the pan from the heat.

Taste-test the sauce and add more salt and pepper, if required (it will probably need more salt). When satisfied with the taste, mix in the cubed butter and stir until melted. Serve immediately.

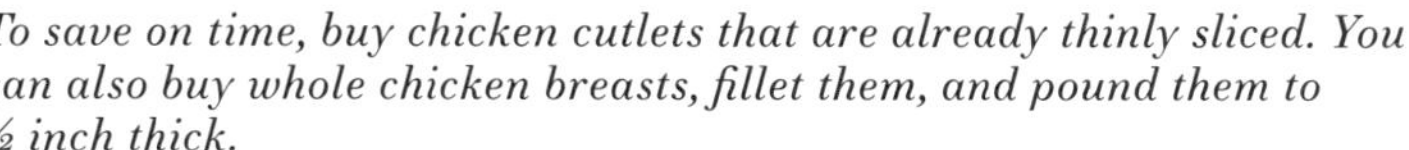

To save on time, buy chicken cutlets that are already thinly sliced. You can also buy whole chicken breasts, fillet them, and pound them to ½ inch thick.

This recipe calls for cremini mushrooms, but you can use any mushrooms available in your local grocery store.

BISTECCA ALLA FIORENTINA

MAKES: 4 SERVINGS • **PREP:** 5 MINUTES • **MARINATE:** 4 HOURS • **COOK:** 20 MINUTES

Bistecca alla Fiorentina, or steak in the Florentine style, may just be one of the best ways to showcase the incredible flavor of steak. With barely any ingredients, the steak is the true star of the show, enhanced only by some salt, olive oil, rosemary, and sage.

Because it can be a challenge to source a 3-inch-thick porterhouse steak in the prepackaged meat section of your grocery store, it's best to visit the butcher counter and ask them to cut it for you. You can also use a tomahawk steak. And while a traditional bistecca Fiorentina is served rare and only uses olive oil, I recommend that you cook it to *your* liking. I'm not going to judge if you want to throw a few tablespoons of butter in the pan right after it comes out of the oven.

This dish is great served with a side of rosemary roasted potatoes or mashed potatoes and a simple green salad.

INGREDIENTS

1 (3-inch-thick) porterhouse steak, about 3 pounds (1.4 kg)

1½ tablespoons (15 g) kosher salt

2 sprigs rosemary

2 bunches sage

2 to 3 tablespoons (30 to 45 ml) extra virgin olive oil

Flaky sea salt, for serving

INSTRUCTIONS

FOR THE PREP

Sprinkle the steak on all sides with the kosher salt and place it on a wire rack set in a baking sheet. Place the steak in the fridge, uncovered, for at least 4 hours but preferably overnight.

FOR COOKING THE STEAK

Take the steak out of the fridge at least 1 hour prior to cooking.

Preheat the oven to 400°F and set the rack to the middle level. Tie the rosemary and sage together.

Heat a large cast iron pan over medium-high heat. Give it time to get very hot.

While the pan is heating up, drizzle the olive oil all over the steak. Use the bundle of herbs to brush the oil evenly over all sides of the steak.

Once the pan is very hot, place the steak in the pan and sear for 3 minutes, then flip it over and sear on the other side for 3 minutes. Using strong tongs, grab the steak and sear it for 1 minute each on the narrow sides, then lay it back down in the pan. Carefully grab the pan with a potholder and remove it from the burner. Place an ovenproof thermometer into the thickest part of the meat. Place the pan in the oven and cook the steak to 110 to 115°F for rare or to your preferred doneness.

Remove the steak, place on a cutting board, and let it rest for 7 to 10 minutes before slicing. To slice, remove both the tenderloin and strip sides and cut into large pieces. Brush the herbs on top of the pieces one more time and sprinkle with flaky sea salt. Serve immediately.

Use an ovenproof thermometer to ensure the steak is cooked to your preferred temperature.

Save the bone and add it to your Sunday sauce (see page 58) for amazing beef flavor!

STEAK PIZZAIOLA

MAKES: 6 SERVINGS • **PREP:** 10 MINUTES • **COOK:** 2 HOURS, 20 MINUTES

Steak pizzaiola, or "pizza maker's steak," was something my mom made often while I was growing up, and the dish can be found in many restaurants in the New York metropolitan area. It's also one of the Italian American dishes made even more famous by Ray Romano, who had an affinity for his mom's steak pizzaiola in his sitcom *Everybody Loves Raymond*.

While many high-end restaurants will use expensive cuts of beef, such as dry-aged ribeyes, I prefer a more economical peasant-style version using chuck steaks. It's not only budget-friendly, but braising the beef in the pizzaiola sauce for a few hours yields super tender meat with tremendous flavor!

Serve this with a side of pasta or crusty bread and some garlicky sautéed greens for a full meal.

INGREDIENTS

- 5 tablespoons (75 ml) extra virgin olive oil, divided
- 4 boneless chuck steaks, about 3 pounds (1.4 kg) in all, pounded ½ inch thick
- Salt and pepper, to taste
- 1 large red bell pepper, sliced
- ½ pound (226 g) cremini mushrooms, sliced
- 15 cloves garlic, chopped
- ¼ teaspoon crushed hot red pepper flakes
- ½ cup (120 ml) dry white wine
- ½ cup (120 ml) low-sodium beef stock
- 1 (28-ounce) can plum tomatoes, hand crushed or pulsed in a blender
- 1 teaspoon dried oregano
- 5 large basil leaves, chopped
- Grated pecorino Romano cheese, for serving

INSTRUCTIONS

Heat 2 tablespoons of the olive oil in a large heavy pan over a touch higher than medium heat. Pat the steaks very dry and liberally season all over with salt and black pepper. Sear the steaks in the hot pan until well browned on both sides, then remove the steaks and place on a plate.

Add the remaining 3 tablespoons of olive oil to the pan along with the bell peppers and mushrooms. Sauté until soft, 7 to 10 minutes, then add the garlic and cook for another 2 minutes or until lightly golden. Add the red pepper flakes and cook for another 30 seconds.

Add the wine and beef stock and bring to a boil while scraping the pan with a wooden spoon to dislodge the brown bits. After 2 minutes reduce the heat to medium-low, add the tomatoes, and stir together. Bring the sauce to a lively simmer. Taste-test and add salt and black pepper to taste along with the oregano.

Return the steaks to the pan and cover. Cook at a low simmer until very tender, 1½ to 2 hours. Flip the steaks every 30 minutes to ensure even cooking. If the sauce starts to dry out during the braising process, just add a little water to the pan.

Once the steaks are very tender, turn off the heat and taste-test one more time, adjusting the salt and pepper if required. There will be a good amount of fat in the sauce that has risen to the top. If you like, you can spoon some of it out.

Top with the basil and serve immediately with pecorino on the side.

Tough cuts of beef like top round and bottom round also work well when pounded thin, though I prefer the fat and flavor profile of chuck steaks. Bone-in chuck steaks also work great for this dish.

If serving with pasta, double the amount of ingredients for the sauce.

It's recommended to use chuck roast since it has a unique fat profile; however, you can also use leaner roasts such as rump roast, top round, or bottom round.

Use kitchen twine to tie up the roast or ask your butcher to tie it for you. Doing so will create a more evenly shaped roast, which allows for even searing and braising.

This recipe includes flour, which helps to thicken the sauce. If you'd like an even thicker sauce, mix 2 tablespoons of cornstarch with ¼ cup of water and add to the simmering sauce. Start by adding only half, and if it's still not thick enough, add the rest.

CLASSIC POT ROAST

MAKES: 6–8 SERVINGS • **PREP:** 10 MINUTES • **COOK:** 4 HOURS, 30 MINUTES

I believe every home cook should have a tried-and-true pot roast recipe they turn to when the weather cools down and comfort food is on the brain.

My classic pot roast recipe combines budget-friendly chuck roast with chunks of carrots and potatoes braised with herbs in a combination of red wine and beef stock. It's not only easy to make, but the methods I highlight below help yield maximum flavor, super tender beef, and the best pot roast sauce you've ever had!

INGREDIENTS

1 (4-pound/1.8 kg) chuck roast, tied (see notes opposite)

2½ teaspoons fine sea salt, plus more to taste

½ teaspoon ground black pepper, plus more to taste

2 tablespoons (30 ml) neutral oil, such as avocado oil

2 cups (480 ml) low-sodium beef stock, divided

¼ cup (60 ml) extra virgin olive oil

2 large onions, cut into large pieces

8 cloves garlic, chopped

3 tablespoons (45 g) tomato paste

¼ cup (32 g) all-purpose flour

1½ cups (360 ml) dry red wine

2 tablespoons (30 ml) Worcestershire sauce

10 sprigs thyme, tied together

2 large bay leaves

1½ pounds (680 g) red or small yellow potatoes, cut into large chunks

2 pounds (908 g) carrots, cut into 3-inch chunks

3 tablespoons minced flat-leaf Italian parsley, for garnish

INSTRUCTIONS

Preheat the oven to 325°F and set the rack to the middle level with enough room to accommodate a Dutch oven and its lid.

Heat a large pan over medium heat. Pat the chuck roast dry with paper towels, then season with salt and pepper. Add the neutral oil to the pan along with the chuck roast. Sear until browned on all sides, about 15 minutes total, then remove the roast and set on a plate.

Add ½ cup of beef stock to the pan and use a wooden spoon to gently dislodge the brown bits from the bottom. Pour the pan sauce into the same vessel as the remaining 1½ cups of beef stock and set aside.

Heat a large Dutch oven over medium heat, add the olive oil and onions along with a pinch of salt, and cook, stirring occasionally, until translucent, about 10 minutes. Add the garlic and cook for another 2 minutes or until fragrant.

Add the tomato paste and cook for 3 minutes, then add the flour and mix until all the white specks have vanished, about 1 minute.

Add the wine, beef stock, Worcestershire sauce, thyme, and bay leaves to the pot and bring to a boil while stirring to break up any flour clumps. Boil for 2 minutes, then turn off the heat, add the roast to the pot, and cover. Place it into the oven to roast.

After 1½ hours, remove the pot and uncover it. Quickly add the potatoes and carrots to the pot and cover again. Return to the oven for another 2 to 2½ hours or until the meat is fork-tender.

Place the pot roast and veggies on a plate covered with tented foil. Remove and discard the bay leaves and thyme.

To degrease the sauce, lay paper towels on top of the sauce to absorb the fat and discard, or use a ladle to skim some of the fat.

The sauce will be quite thick from the added flour, but for an even thicker sauce, simply use an immersion blender to blend the softened onions and a few potatoes. Alternatively, heat just the pot with the sauce over medium-high heat to reduce until the sauce coats the back of a wooden spoon.

The roast can be shredded or cut into chunks and mixed with the sauce. Any large pieces of fat can be discarded right before serving. Season the carrots and potatoes with salt and pepper to taste and garnish with the parsley. Serve immediately.

PRIME RIB AU JUS

MAKES: 6 SERVINGS • **PREP:** 20 MINUTES • **DRY BRINE:** OVERNIGHT • **COOK:** 3 HOURS, 30 MINUTES

I've been making prime rib on Christmas Day for over 20 years, and the low and slow method I outline below is everything you need to make a juicy medium-rare prime rib roast and the best au jus.

Because prime rib is a more expensive cut of beef, it is usually reserved for holidays and special occasions; however, I encourage you to make this whenever you want. We shouldn't have to relegate our favorite foods to one day a year!

Prime rib is best served with a side of roasted or mashed potatoes, creamed spinach, and Yorkshire pudding or dinner rolls.

FOR THE PRIME RIB

- 1 (6-pound/2.7 kg) prime rib or beef rib roast, rib bones removed, then tied back on (ask the butcher)
- 3 tablespoons (30 g) kosher salt
- 1 tablespoon (8 g) coarsely ground black pepper

FOR THE JUS

- 3 tablespoons (45 ml) olive oil
- 3 pounds (1.4 kg) oxtails, neck bones, or other meaty beef bones
- 2 large carrots, chopped
- 3 celery ribs, chopped
- 1 large onion, chopped
- 1 tablespoon (15 g) tomato paste
- 5 cloves garlic
- 6 cups (1.4 L) low-sodium beef stock
- ½ cup (120 ml) dry red wine
- 1 teaspoon Better than Bouillon beef base (see notes opposite)
- 2 sprigs thyme
- 1 large bay leaf
- Salt and pepper, to taste

FOR THE PRIME RIB

Season the roast with the salt and pepper on all sides, then place on a wire rack–lined baking sheet and refrigerate uncovered overnight.

Three hours before cooking, remove the prime rib from the fridge.

When you're ready to cook, preheat the oven to 250°F and set the rack to the middle level. Place a digital probe into the center of the roast and set it to go off at 115°F.

Place the roast in the oven and cook until it achieves 115°F (anywhere from 2½ to 3½ hours), then lightly tent the roast with foil and let rest for 30 minutes. While the roast cooks, make the jus.

FOR THE JUS

Heat a large heavy pot or Dutch oven over medium heat. Add the olive oil to the pot. Dry the bones with paper towels, then add them to the pot and brown on all sides, about 10 minutes.

Add the carrots, celery, onion, tomato paste, and a pinch of salt to the pot and cook for 10 minutes, stirring occasionally until soft, then add the garlic and cook for another 1 to 2 minutes.

Add the beef stock, wine, beef base, thyme, and bay leaf to the pot and bring to a boil. Dislodge all of the brown bits from the bottom of the pot by scraping with a wooden spoon. Once boiling, lower to a simmer and cook uncovered until the roast is finished.

FOR FINISHING

Set one oven rack to the lowest level and line it with foil (to prevent drippings from smoking and setting off the fire alarm). Set the second rack to the middle level and turn on the broiler.

Broil the roast on the middle level until well browned on all sides, about 2 minutes per side (use tongs to turn), then remove from the oven and set it on a carving board. Strain the jus through a fine-mesh strainer, then discard the solids. Add a ladle of the jus to the roasting pan to deglaze by scraping with a wooden spoon to dislodge any brown bits, then pour the drippings from the roasting pan into the jus. Taste-test and season with salt and pepper before serving with the prime rib. Remove the strings and bones and slice the roast into pieces. Enjoy!

To save some work, ask your butcher to remove the bones and tie them back to the roast.

If using homemade beef stock, use only 1 teaspoon of beef base. If not using homemade stock, use 6 cups of mixed beef stock from reduced-sodium Better Than Bouillon beef base.

The process of broiling the roast on all sides can create smoke, so be aware that it may set off a smoke alarm. Lining the bottom rack of the oven with foil to catch any fat can help mitigate this. Alternatively, if you have access to an outdoor grill, you can use the grill to sear the roast on all sides instead of using the broiler.

Use an ovenproof digital meat thermometer to ensure the prime rib is cooked perfectly to your liking. The exact cooking time will vary based on the size of the roast. For an almost 7-pound roast, it took us exactly 3 hours to cook it to 115°F. The carryover cooking during resting, along with the broiling process, brought the roast to a final temperature of 130°F, medium-rare. If you like your roast more on the rare side, cook initially to less than 115°F, or cook to a higher temperature if you like it more well-done.

SIP & FEAST TIPS

Our family prefers flank steak, but you can use skirt, ribeye, or filet mignon as well.

Be sure to slice the steak into bite-sized pieces against the grain to ensure the most tender bite.

While you can certainly make this dish without the marinade, I urge you not to skip this step. The marinade adds tremendous flavor. If you're short on time, you can reduce the marinating time to 10 minutes.

Be sure to reserve your pasta water, as it is an essential part of this dish.

BEEF STROGANOFF

MAKES: 6–8 SERVINGS • **PREP:** 10 MINUTES • **MARINATE:** 2 HOURS • **COOK:** 35 MINUTES

This hearty combination of seared steak and mushrooms in a creamy, tangy sauce is pure comfort food. Ingredients like allspice and nutmeg increase the coziness factor of this dish and make it taste as though it took all day to make, but in reality it comes together quite quickly, making it great for weeknights.

FOR THE SEARED STEAK

1½ pounds (680 g) flank steak

1 tablespoon (15 ml) Worcestershire sauce

2 teaspoons ground allspice

½ teaspoon ground nutmeg

1 teaspoon fine sea salt

¼ teaspoon ground black pepper

2 tablespoons (30 ml) neutral oil, such as avocado oil

½ cup (120 ml) low-sodium beef stock

FOR THE STROGANOFF

6 tablespoons (90 ml) extra virgin olive oil, divided

1½ pounds (680 g) cremini mushrooms, thickly sliced

Salt and pepper, to taste

6 tablespoons (84 g) butter, divided

2 medium onions, sliced

6 cloves garlic, minced

1 pound (454 g) wide egg noodles

¼ cup (32 g) all-purpose flour

2½ cups (600 ml) low-sodium beef stock

½ cup (120 ml) dry white wine

2 tablespoons (30 g) Dijon mustard

2 tablespoons (30 ml) Worcestershire sauce

½ cup (120 ml) heavy cream

½ cup (120 g) sour cream

2 tablespoons minced flat-leaf Italian parsley, optional

FOR THE SEARED STEAK

Slice the steak into 2-inch-wide strips with the grain, then slice into thin bite-sized pieces against the grain. Place the meat into a large bowl and mix well with the Worcestershire sauce, allspice, nutmeg, salt, and pepper. Refrigerate for at least 2 hours, or up to overnight, before searing the beef. If you're short on time, you can reduce the marinating time to 10 minutes.

Heat a large pan over medium-high heat and add the oil. Sear the steak for 2 to 3 minutes or until browned. Remove the steak pieces to a dish and tent with foil to keep warm. Pour the ½ cup beef stock into the pan and gently scrape the bottom of the pan to dislodge any brown bits. Combine the pan juices with the 2½ cups beef stock for the stroganoff and set aside.

FOR THE STROGANOFF

Bring a large pot of salted water to boil.

Heat the same large pan you used for the steak over medium heat and add 3 tablespoons of the olive oil and the mushrooms. Cook the mushrooms, stirring occasionally, until they release their water and brown, 7 to 10 minutes, then season with salt and pepper to taste and move them to a bowl.

Add the remaining 3 tablespoons of olive oil, 3 tablespoons of the butter, and the onions to the pan and sauté until soft, about 10 minutes. Add the garlic and cook for another 2 minutes or until very fragrant.

Begin cooking the egg noodles according to the package instructions.

Add the flour to the pan and cook for 1 minute or until all the white specks are gone.

Add the beef stock mixture and wine to the pan and turn the heat to high. With a flat wooden spoon, scrape the bottom of the pan to dislodge all the brown bits.

Bring to a boil while whisking until smooth for 3 minutes. Lower the heat to a simmer and add the cooked mushrooms, sliced steak, mustard, and Worcestershire sauce to the pan. Continue to cook at a low simmer while waiting for the noodles.

When the noodles are finished, drain, reserving about 2 cups (480 ml) of the pasta water. Toss the egg noodles with the remaining 3 tablespoons of butter.

Add the heavy cream and sour cream to the pan and continue to simmer for 2 minutes. Taste the sauce and adjust the salt and pepper, if required. If the sauce is too thick, add a little of the reserved pasta water at a time to get the consistency just right. When satisfied, remove the pan from the heat.

Divide the noodles among bowls and ladle the stroganoff over each one. Garnish with the parsley and serve immediately.

BRACIOLE

MAKES: 4–6 SERVINGS • **PREP:** 30 MINUTES • **COOK:** 2 HOURS, 30 MINUTES TO 3 HOURS, 30 MINUTES

There is no better addition to Sunday sauce than beef braciole! Most Italian American families have their own beloved version. My version is more Sicilian influenced, using pignoli nuts and raisins..

Braciole is most often cooked in tomato sauce for hours, ergo the Sunday sauce reference. While it is definitely the star of the show, it can be cooked alongside meatballs and other cuts of meat (see Rigatoni with Sunday Sauce on page 58 for more information), and it is almost always served with pasta.

FOR THE SAUCE

- ¼ cup (60 ml) extra virgin olive oil
- 1 medium onion, diced
- 5 cloves garlic, minced
- 2 tablespoons (30 g) tomato paste
- ½ cup (120 ml) dry red wine
- 3 (28-ounce) cans plum tomatoes, hand crushed or pulsed in a blender
- Salt and pepper, to taste
- ½ cup (120 ml) water, plus more as needed

FOR THE BRACIOLE

- ¼ cup (60 ml) extra virgin olive oil
- 3 cloves garlic, mashed into a paste
- ¼ cup (35 g) pignoli nuts
- 1 cup (100 g) plain breadcrumbs
- ½ cup minced flat-leaf Italian parsley
- ¼ cup (42 g) raisins or currants, soaked in water for 10 minutes, then drained
- ½ cup (45 g) grated pecorino Romano cheese
- 2 pounds (908 g) top round
- Salt and pepper, to taste
- Olive oil, for shallow frying
- ½ cup (120 ml) dry red wine, optional (see notes opposite)

FOR THE SAUCE

Heat the olive oil in a large pot over a touch less than medium heat. Add the onion and cook, stirring occasionally, until soft, 7 to 10 minutes, then add the garlic and cook for another 2 minutes or until fragrant.

Add the tomato paste and cook for 5 minutes, spreading the paste around with a wooden spoon. If it starts to burn, add a little water. Add the wine and cook for 2 minutes while scraping the bottom of the pan to dislodge any brown bits.

Add the plum tomatoes and water and bring to a simmer. Once simmering, partially cover and lower the heat to the lowest level, so that the sauce is barely bubbling. You can season with a touch of salt right now, but it's best to wait, because the sauce will reduce and concentrate.

FOR THE BRACIOLE

Heat the extra virgin olive oil in a small pan over medium heat and add the garlic. Once lightly golden, add the pignoli nuts and cook for 1 to 2 minutes until golden. Add the breadcrumbs, parsley, and raisins. Mix well until a paste forms. Remove the pan from the heat, mix in the pecorino, and set aside.

Carefully slice the top round lengthwise into 2 or 3 pieces roughly ½ inch thick. Cut the beef into approximately 3-x-4-inch rectangles. Pound each rectangle to roughly ¼ inch thick, which will make them substantially larger.

Arrange the pounded meat on a cutting board and season with salt and pepper. Leaving some space around the edges, evenly spread the paste onto each piece. You should have a thin layer of the mixture on each piece of meat. Roll each piece tightly and secure them with toothpicks or kitchen twine.

Heat the olive oil in a large pan over a touch less than medium heat. Sear the braciole on all sides, working in batches if required to avoid overcrowding the pan.

After the braciole are seared, add each one to the pot of sauce. If the pan isn't burned, pour off the fat from the pan and deglaze with the wine. Scrape the brown bits off the bottom of the pan, pour the pan juices into the pot of sauce, and mix to incorporate.

Cook for 2 to 3 hours or until fork-tender over very low heat partially covered, making sure to stir the sauce occasionally. If the sauce dries out during the cooking process, add ½ cup of water or more as needed. Alternatively, if your pot is ovenproof, you can cover it and place it in the center of the oven at 300°F for 2 to 3 hours or until tender.

Once tender, remove the braciole from the sauce and remove the toothpicks. Taste-test the sauce and season with salt and pepper. Serve with pasta, grated cheese, and crusty bread, if desired.

Bottom round, eye of round, flank steak, or sirloin can be used in place of the top round. They should all be pounded flat to ¼ inch thick for easy rolling. Often your butcher can do this for you. Also, beef will sometimes be sold already pounded thin and labeled "for braciole or involtini" at Italian specialty stores.

Kitchen twine will hold the braciole more securely, but toothpicks work well and are far easier to remove.

Beef braciole is not something to be rushed. Because we're using a tougher cut of meat, cooking it requires time to tenderize and break down the connective tissue. It's best to start your braciole early in the day and allow it to cook in the sauce for several hours on a very low simmer.

After the braciole are seared I like to deglaze the pan with some red wine, then add the mixture to the sauce. This enhances the flavor, but isn't required and should only be done if the pan drippings are brown. If they're black, they're burned and should not be added to the sauce.

PORK CHOPS AND VINEGAR PEPPERS

MAKES: 6 SERVINGS • **PREP:** 5 MINUTES • **COOK:** 1 HOUR, 40 MINUTES

I've been eating and making pork chops with vinegar peppers, also known as cherry peppers, for years, and have always loved it! If you're a fan of *The Sopranos*, you may have noticed this dish made an appearance in the "Live Free or Die" episode, where Vito makes it for Johnnycakes and describes it as "real peasant food." And I can see why—pork chops are still relatively inexpensive, especially if you're using blade or shoulder chops, as are jarred vinegar peppers. Together they create a winning combination with outrageous flavor!

We typically eat this dish with a side of roasted potatoes, crusty bread, and sautéed broccoli rabe.

INGREDIENTS

¼ cup (60 ml) extra virgin olive oil, divided

6 (1-inch-thick) bone-in pork chops (see notes below)

Salt and pepper, to taste

10 cloves garlic

4 large pickled cherry peppers, chopped (seeds and stems removed), plus more for serving

¾ cup (180 ml) dry white wine

¾ cup (180 ml) low-sodium chicken stock

¼ cup (60 ml) pickling liquid from cherry pepper jar

¼ cup minced flat-leaf Italian parsley

INSTRUCTIONS

Heat 2 tablespoons of the olive oil in a large pan over medium-high heat. Pat the pork chops dry and season well with salt and pepper on both sides. Add the chops to the pan and sear until browned on both sides, about 3 minutes per side. Remove the chops and set on a plate covered with tented foil.

Lower the heat to medium and add the garlic and the remaining 2 tablespoons of olive oil. Sauté until the garlic is golden, 1 to 2 minutes.

Next, add the cherry peppers and stir. Add the wine, stock, and pickling liquid and turn the heat to high. Bring the sauce to a boil for 2 minutes, then lower the heat down to medium-low.

Nestle the pork chops into the sauce, then cover and simmer for 1 to 1½ hours or until the pork is very tender. Every 20 to 30 minutes, turn the chops over to achieve even cooking.

Mix the parsley into the sauce. Serve the pork with sauce spooned over the top of each chop.

A standard blade chop will take over an hour to braise and become tender, while premium pork chops, such as loin chops, can just be pan-seared. If using a premium pork chop, you can sear the chops to medium or cook them on the grill, then cover with the sauce at the end. These would not require the same level of braising as other chops.

Cherry peppers are a bit spicy, so if you don't enjoy heat you can use sweet vinegar peppers instead.

If the sauce evaporates toward the end of the braising process, add ½ cup of water and stir to combine.

SIP & FEAST TIPS

TUSCAN-STYLE BALSAMIC-GLAZED RIBS

MAKES: 4–6 SERVINGS • **PREP:** 15 MINUTES • **COOK:** 2 HOURS, 45 MINUTES • **MARINATE:** 1 HOUR

I've been making barbecued ribs for decades now, usually in my outdoor smoker, but when the weather turns cold, I opt for these delicious oven-baked Tuscan-style ribs. Using an oven makes the process so much easier and since they're cooked low and slow, they are super tender and easy to eat.

They're finished with a balsamic glaze that's just a little sweet but adds tremendous flavor and just the right amount of stickiness we all want when we dig into some ribs. These are great with a side of roasted garlic mashed potatoes or roasted potatoes and garlicky sautéed spinach.

FOR THE RIBS

- 2 racks baby back ribs, about 4 pounds (1.8 kg)
- 4 teaspoons (13 g) kosher salt
- 1 tablespoon fennel seeds
- 1 teaspoon dried rosemary leaves
- 1 teaspoon smoked paprika
- 1 teaspoon onion powder
- 1 teaspoon black peppercorns
- ½ teaspoon ground cinnamon

FOR THE GLAZE

- 1¼ cups (300 ml) balsamic vinegar
- ½ cup (120 ml) water
- ¼ cup (60 ml) honey
- 1 sprig rosemary
- Salt and pepper, to taste

FOR THE RIBS

Dry the ribs with paper towels. If the membrane has not already been removed, use a paper towel to grab and pull it off (see notes opposite).

Place the salt, fennel seeds, rosemary, paprika, onion powder, peppercorns, and cinnamon into a spice or coffee grinder and pulverize to a fine powder. Rub the spice mixture evenly on both sides of the ribs. Wrap the ribs in foil and place them on a foil-lined baking sheet. Refrigerate for at least 1 hour, but preferably overnight.

Preheat the oven to 250°F and set the rack to the middle level.

Bake the ribs for 2½ hours, then check for tenderness. If the ribs aren't tender, close the foil and bake for another 30 minutes and check again. Once the ribs are tender, remove them from the oven.

FOR THE GLAZE

Meanwhile, combine the vinegar, water, honey, and rosemary in a small saucepan and bring to a boil while stirring to incorporate. Once boiling, lower the heat to a simmer and cook until the glaze has thickened and reduced by roughly half. Remove and discard the rosemary sprig and taste-test the glaze. Season with salt and pepper as needed.

FOR FINISHING

Turn on the broiler and set the rack to the second-highest level.

Unwrap the ribs and place them on the foil-lined baking sheet. Pat the ribs dry of any accumulated juices, then baste with the glaze on both sides. Broil for 1 to 3 minutes per side, watching carefully for burning! Remove the ribs from the oven and slice. Spread the glaze over the ribs, then serve with any remaining glaze on the side.

To remove the membrane from the ribs, position the ribs bone side up on a cutting board. Starting at one side of the rack, slide a butter knife under the silver skin to loosen it. With paper towels, grab the loosened silver skin and pull off the membrane across the whole rack.

Allowing the ribs to sit with the rub for at least 1 hour, but preferably overnight, in the fridge will yield maximum flavor.

If you like a lot of sauce, you can easily double the glaze so there's plenty left for serving with the ribs.

Between the balsamic vinegar and the honey, the glaze has a good amount of sugar so it can caramelize and burn easily when under the broiler. Be sure to watch the ribs carefully during the broiling stage and remove them from the oven if needed.

We use bulk sausage for this recipe, but if you can't find it, use sausage links. Simply make a slit down the middle of each link and release the sausage from the casing. Use whatever type of sausage you prefer; hot, fennel, etc.

It's so important to season the inside of the peppers prior to stuffing them. It's a simple, quick step, but don't skip it. Your stuffed peppers will taste vastly better if you season them first with salt and pepper.

Make sure you get a good seal when prepping the peppers to go into the oven. We use parchment paper first to prevent the cheese from sticking, and then foil. The tight seal on the foil will help the peppers steam and soften. Additionally, cutting a tiny hole in the bottom of each pepper will allow the steam inside the pepper to release and prevent them from bursting. These may seem like small steps but they do make a difference!

STUFFED CUBANELLE PEPPERS

MAKES: 4–6 SERVINGS • **PREP:** 20 MINUTES • **COOK:** 1 HOUR, 30 MINUTES

Stuffed peppers and other stuffed veggies are always a hit in our home. They're rich in flavor and texture, simple to make, and filling enough to count as a complete meal. We make some variation of stuffed peppers pretty regularly, and this version uses Cubanelles, also known as Italian frying peppers.

We use arborio rice; however, any white rice will work for this recipe. Stuffed Cubanelles are the perfect opportunity to use leftover rice, whether it's homemade rice or even takeout rice, harkening back to the "waste not, want not" idea. Both my grandmother and mother bestowed that mentality on me at an early age, and I couldn't be more grateful!

While stuffed peppers really are a complete meal, meaning no sides needed, a salad to finish the meal couldn't hurt.

INGREDIENTS

1 pound (454 g) bulk mild Italian sausage

2 tablespoons (30 ml) extra virgin olive oil

1 medium onion, diced

6 cloves garlic, minced

¼ teaspoon crushed hot red pepper flakes, optional

1½ cups (170 g) shredded whole-milk block mozzarella cheese, divided

1½ cups (300 g) cooked arborio rice, or plain white rice

½ cup (45 g) grated pecorino Romano cheese

¼ cup minced flat-leaf Italian parsley

5 cups (1.2 L) marinara sauce (see page 57), divided

1 cup (240 ml) water

8 large Cubanelle peppers, tops cut off and seeds removed

Salt and pepper, to taste

INSTRUCTIONS

Preheat the oven to 350°F and set the rack to the middle level. In a large pan, sauté the sausage over medium heat until browned, 7 to 10 minutes, then transfer to a plate and set aside.

Turn the heat down to medium-low. Add the olive oil and onion to the pan and sauté for 3 to 5 minutes until softened, then add the garlic and continue to cook for 2 to 3 minutes longer. If desired, add the red pepper flakes and cook for 30 seconds.

Remove the pan from the heat and stir in the sausage, ¾ cup of the mozzarella, the rice, pecorino, parsley, and ½ cup of the marinara sauce. Mix well and set the stuffing aside.

Pour enough of the remaining marinara sauce to come ½ inch high in a large baking dish, add the water, and mix together.

Season the interior of each pepper with salt and pepper. Stuff the peppers with the rice mixture and place them lying flat in the baking dish. Add a thin layer of sauce to top of the peppers and sprinkle the remaining ¾ cup of mozzarella cheese on top.

Make a few holes in the side of each pepper with a knife or toothpick. This will prevent the peppers from bursting as they cook. Tightly cover the baking dish with parchment paper, then aluminum foil, and bake for 1 hour.

Remove the foil and parchment and check the peppers. If they are tender, you can remove them from the oven, or recover and continue cooking for 10 to 15 minutes longer if necessary. If you like, you can remove the cover and broil the top for 30 to 60 seconds before serving, but watch carefully. Allow the peppers to sit for a few minutes before serving.

SHRIMP OREGANATA

MAKES: 4–6 SERVINGS • **PREP:** 10 MINUTES • **COOK:** 14 MINUTES

Shrimp oreganata is a dish I grew up eating, and it can be found at many restaurants in the New York metropolitan area. It's loaded with outrageous flavor from the garlic, breadcrumbs, oregano, and white wine, which happens to pair particularly well with seafood in general, like our Baked Clams (page 34).

The beauty of shrimp oreganata is that the recipe is totally customizable. If you want more garlic, add it; don't want wine, omit it. It really is that simple. We usually serve shrimp oreganata as a main course with a side of rice and sautéed greens, but you could also offer this dish as an appetizer. And it goes without saying that this is a must-make for Christmas Eve's Feast of the Seven Fishes!

FOR THE SEASONED BREADCRUMBS

- 3 tablespoons (45 ml) extra virgin olive oil
- 6 cloves garlic, minced
- ⅓ cup (33 g) plain breadcrumbs
- 2 tablespoons (16 g) grated Parmigiano-Reggiano cheese
- 2 tablespoons minced flat-leaf Italian parsley
- 1 tablespoon (15 ml) fresh lemon juice
- 2 teaspoons dried oregano
- ½ teaspoon crushed hot red pepper flakes
- ½ teaspoon kosher salt

FOR THE SHRIMP

- 1½ pounds (680 g) colossal shrimp, peeled and deveined (12–15 count)
- Salt and pepper, to taste
- ¾ cup (180 ml) low-sodium chicken stock
- ¼ cup (60 ml) dry white wine
- 6 tablespoons (84 g) butter, cubed
- 3 tablespoons (45 ml) extra virgin olive oil, as needed
- 1 large lemon, cut into wedges, for serving

FOR THE SEASONED BREADCRUMBS

Heat the olive oil in a large pan over medium-low heat and sauté the garlic for 2 minutes or until fragrant. Add the remaining breadcrumb ingredients and mix well. Turn off the heat and set aside.

FOR THE SHRIMP

Preheat the oven to 425°F. Set one rack in the middle and the other rack near the top of the oven.

Pat the shrimp very dry, then season with salt and pepper to taste.

In an ovenproof baking dish or large pan, arrange the shrimp with tails pointing up. Distribute the seasoned breadcrumbs on top of the shrimp.

Pour the chicken stock and wine around the shrimp and sprinkle the cubed butter all over and into the sauce. Drizzle approximately 2 tablespoons of extra virgin olive oil all over the breadcrumbs, or more if needed to thoroughly moisten them.

Bake for 10 minutes or until the shrimp are just about cooked through.

After 10 minutes, move the baking dish to the top rack and broil for 1 to 2 minutes or until nice and brown. Remove the shrimp from the oven and plate with the lemon wedges. Spoon the sauce onto the plates and serve with crusty bread, if desired, to mop up all of the butter sauce.

The breadcrumbs in this dish should be well moistened, and there's no need to overdo it with them as the sauce may become too thick or dry out. If that happens, add some water to loosen it up before serving.

Broiling at the end isn't mandatory, but is suggested, as it will give a wonderful toasty top to the breadcrumbs. When broiling, watch carefully to prevent burning.

SHRIMP SAGANAKI

MAKES: 4–6 SERVINGS • **PREP:** 10 MINUTES • **BRINE:** 10 MINUTES • **COOK:** 30 MINUTES

I have always loved Greek food, but it wasn't until recently that I made shrimp saganaki and knew I had to add the recipe to this cookbook. It combines succulent shrimp with tomatoes, olives, and feta that's baked until bubbly and absolutely bursting with Mediterranean flavor.

I make it as a main course for my family, but it can also be enjoyed as an appetizer. Serve it alongside warm pitas, orzo, or rice pilaf for a complete and delicious meal.

INGREDIENTS

2 pounds (908 g) extra-large shrimp, peeled and deveined (26 count or larger)

½ cup (120 ml) extra virgin olive oil, divided

1 teaspoon kosher salt

½ teaspoon baking soda

¾ teaspoon crushed hot red pepper flakes, divided

1 medium onion, diced

8 cloves garlic, sliced

¼ cup (60 ml) ouzo, or ½ cup (120 ml) dry white wine

1 (14-ounce) can diced tomatoes

¾ pound (340 g) cherry tomatoes, halved

1 tablespoon (15 ml) honey

2 teaspoons dried Greek oregano

Salt and pepper, to taste

¾ cup (180 g) feta cheese, plus more for serving

⅓ cup (47 g) kalamata olives, pitted

¼ cup minced flat-leaf Italian parsley

1 large lemon, cut into wedges, for serving

INSTRUCTIONS

Dry the shrimp with paper towels, place in a large bowl, and mix with 2 tablespoons of the olive oil, the salt, baking soda, and ¼ teaspoon of the red pepper flakes. Let the shrimp sit for at least 10 minutes before searing.

Heat a large, ovenproof cast iron or stainless steel pan over a touch higher than medium heat. Add another 2 tablespoons of the olive oil. Once the oil is shimmering, add the shrimp and cook for 30 seconds per side, working in batches to avoid overcrowding the pan. Place the seared shrimp on a plate covered with tented foil.

Set the oven rack to the second-highest level and preheat the broiler.

Heat the same pan used to sear the shrimp over medium heat and add the remaining ¼ cup of olive oil and the onion. Cook the onion until soft, stirring occasionally for about 7 minutes, then add the garlic and cook for another 1 to 2 minutes or until fragrant.

Add ½ teaspoon of the red pepper flakes and cook for 30 seconds, then add the ouzo and bring to a boil. Once the ouzo has mostly evaporated, add the canned and cherry tomatoes and bring the sauce to a lively simmer. Add the honey and oregano and continue to simmer the sauce to evaporate some of the liquid, 5 to 10 minutes. Taste the sauce and season with salt and pepper if required. Don't go heavy on the salt, though, because a lot of feta and olives are about to get added!

Add the seared shrimp to the sauce and top with the feta cheese and kalamata olives. Broil for approximately 6 minutes or until the shrimp are cooked through and the cheese has started to melt.

Remove from the oven and top with the parsley. Spoon the shrimp and sauce onto plates and serve with the lemon wedges and pita bread, if desired, to mop up all the delicious sauce.

Be sure to use a pan that is ovenproof. The beauty of shrimp saganaki is that it's cooked in one pan, then popped under the broiler to finish and allow the feta to melt and form a creamy and delicious sauce.

Pernod can be subbed for ouzo in the same proportions.

The shrimp only need to be seared for 30 seconds per side in the beginning because they'll finish cooking under the broiler.

Since olives and feta are both salty, be careful when adding any additional salt.

MEDITERRANEAN SALMON

MAKES: 4 SERVINGS • **PREP:** 20 MINUTES • **COOK:** 20 MINUTES

When I'm looking for a quick and easy but still nutritious and tasty meal, I frequently turn to salmon dishes. Salmon is actually great on its own, broiled or baked with just a little salt and pepper and maybe a squeeze of lemon, and that's often how I'll make it for our family. But other times I want to jazz things up and that is how this recipe came to be.

This delicious dish combines some of our favorite Mediterranean ingredients, like capers, olives, and artichoke hearts, in a super-quick sauce that's spooned over the baked salmon. It's great served warm but is also excellent cold!

INGREDIENTS

- 4 (8-ounce/227 g) salmon fillets
- 6 tablespoons (90 ml) extra virgin olive oil, divided
- Salt and pepper, to taste
- 6 cloves garlic, sliced
- ¼ teaspoon crushed hot red pepper flakes
- 3 large plum tomatoes, seeds removed, diced
- 1 (15-ounce) can artichoke hearts, drained, rinsed, and halved
- ½ cup (70 g) pitted kalamata olives, rinsed
- 2 tablespoons (18 g) capers, rinsed
- ¾ cup (180 ml) low-sodium chicken stock
- ¼ cup minced flat-leaf Italian parsley

INSTRUCTIONS

Preheat the oven to 425°F and set the rack to the middle level.

Place the salmon fillets on a parchment paper–lined baking sheet. Drizzle a total of 2 tablespoons of extra virgin olive oil onto the salmon and season with salt and pepper. Bake until cooked through and the salmon reaches an internal temperature of 145°F, 15 to 20 minutes depending on the thickness.

Heat the remaining ¼ cup of olive oil in a large pan over medium heat. Add the garlic and cook, stirring occasionally, until golden, 1 to 2 minutes. Add the red pepper flakes and cook for another 30 seconds.

Add the tomatoes, artichoke hearts, olives, capers, and chicken stock and bring to a lively simmer. Once the liquid reduces by half and starts to thicken, turn the heat to low while waiting for the salmon.

Once the salmon has finished, add the fillets to the pan (or to a platter) and spoon the sauce over the salmon. Turn off the heat and mix in the parsley. Serve either hot or cold.

Canned artichoke hearts often come whole. Simply cut them into halves or quarters. You can also use frozen artichoke hearts, but be sure to thaw them before using.

Capers and olives are very salty so be sure to rinse them before using.

SIP & FEAST TIPS &

Cod is widely available in most grocery stores, but if you can't find it, you can substitute pollack or haddock.

Cut any large pieces of the cod into 6- to 8-inch-long pieces; you should have 4 to 6 pieces in all.

Cod is on the delicate side, so flip it gently when pan-searing it and be sure to use an adequate amount of oil and butter for each batch of cod. Use a nonstick pan for best results.

COD PICCATA

MAKES: 4 SERVINGS • **PREP:** 5 MINUTES • **COOK:** 25 MINUTES

Piccata is one of the best ways to prepare food, because it's so loaded with flavor you'd never know how easy it is! For this dish, the cod is pan-seared and topped with a buttery combination of garlic, capers, and lemon, and comes together in about 30 minutes.

This recipe calls for fresh cod, which is so mild in flavor it can be enjoyed by those who are on the pickier side when it comes to seafood. We usually serve this with some garlicky sautéed spinach and rice.

INGREDIENTS

1½ pounds (680 g) cod fillets

1 teaspoon kosher salt, plus more to taste

¼ teaspoon ground black pepper, plus more to taste

¾ cup (97 g) all-purpose flour, as needed

¼ cup (60 ml) olive oil, as needed

5 tablespoons (70 g) butter, cubed and divided

4 cloves garlic, sliced

3 tablespoons (27 g) capers, rinsed

1 cup (240 ml) low-sodium chicken stock

⅓ cup (80 ml) dry white wine

1 large lemon, cut into 8 slices

Lemon wedges, for serving

3 tablespoons minced flat-leaf Italian parsley

INSTRUCTIONS

Preheat the oven to 325°F and set a rack to the middle level.

Trim any large cod fillets into approximately 6-to-8-inch-long pieces. Pat the fillets dry with paper towels and season both sides of all pieces with the salt and pepper.

Dredge the cod pieces in the flour and set aside on a piece of parchment paper. Save the flour for use later in the recipe.

Heat a large nonstick pan over a touch less than medium heat, then add 1 tablespoon of the olive oil and 1 tablespoon of the butter to the pan. Sear the fillets in the pan, working in batches to avoid crowding and using a bit more olive oil and butter as required to lubricate the pan for each batch, until cooked through, 3 to 4 minutes per side. Set the fillets aside on a platter and cover with tented foil.

After all the cod pieces have been cooked, place the platter in the oven and turn the heat off. This will keep the cod warm while you make the sauce.

Place the same pan you used for the cod over low heat and add the garlic and a touch more olive oil. Sauté the garlic until golden, 1 to 2 minutes, then add the capers and cook for 1 minute more.

Add the chicken stock and wine to the pan and turn the heat to high. With a wooden spoon dislodge all of the brown bits from the bottom of the pan. Boil for 2 to 3 minutes or until the sauce reduces by about half. Turn the heat down to a simmer and add the lemon slices. Simmer the sauce for 2 more minutes.

Roll the remaining butter cubes (about 3 tablespoons worth) in the remaining flour and add them to the pan, one at a time. Using a whisk or wooden spoon, stir the sauce to emulsify. Taste-test and adjust the salt and pepper if required. If a stronger lemon flavor is desired, squeeze a wedge or two into the sauce and taste again.

When satisfied with the taste of the sauce, add the parsley, then remove the platter from the oven and pour the sauce over the cod fillets. Serve with the remaining lemon wedges.

FRIED FLOUNDER WITH HOMEMADE TARTAR SAUCE

MAKES: 6–8 SERVINGS • **PREP:** 10 MINUTES • **COOK:** 25 MINUTES

Fried flounder is one of the easiest dishes you can make. The seasoned breadcrumb coating is crisp, while the inside stays perfectly flaky and moist. All it needs is a squeeze of lemon, but I'm including my homemade tartar sauce recipe here too because it really adds to the fish.

Flounder is widely available where we live on Long Island, but if you can't find flounder, you can easily substitute another white fish, like sole. This is a great one for any night of the week, but it is especially good for Fridays in Lent. These also make a mean fish sandwich!

FOR THE SEASONED BREADCRUMBS

2 cups (200 g) plain breadcrumbs

¼ cup minced flat-leaf Italian parsley

1½ teaspoons dried oregano

1 teaspoon fine sea salt

½ teaspoon ground black pepper

¼ teaspoon garlic powder

FOR THE FLOUNDER

Neutral oil, for frying

1½ pounds (680 g) flounder fillets

Salt and pepper, to taste

½ cup (65 g) all-purpose flour, for dredging

3 large eggs, beaten

Lemon wedges, for serving

FOR THE TARTAR SAUCE (OPTIONAL)

1 cup (240 ml) mayonnaise

¼ cup (60 ml) relish

2 tablespoons (18 g) capers, drained, rinsed, and mashed into a paste

1½ tablespoons (23 ml) fresh lemon juice

1 teaspoon Dijon mustard

5 drops Tabasco sauce, or to taste

Salt and pepper, to taste

FOR THE SEASONED BREADCRUMBS

Mix all the breadcrumb ingredients together in a medium bowl and set aside.

FOR THE FLOUNDER

Fill a heavy pan with ½ inch of oil and heat to 360 to 370°F.

While the oil heats, dry the fish fillets with paper towels and season with salt and pepper on both sides. Line a baking sheet with parchment paper and set aside.

Place the flour and eggs in separate medium bowls alongside the bowl of seasoned breadcrumbs. Dredge a flounder fillet in the flour and shake off the excess. Place the floured fillet into the eggs and coat well on both sides. Finally, place the fillet into the breadcrumbs, making sure to coat well on both sides. Set the fillet on the parchment-lined baking sheet. Repeat the process for the remaining flounder.

Once the oil reaches the proper frying temperature, fry the fish in batches until golden and cooked through, 3 to 4 minutes per side. Do not crowd the pan. Set the fried flounder onto a wire rack or paper towel–lined plates. Serve with the lemon wedges and tartar sauce, if using.

FOR THE TARTAR SAUCE (OPTIONAL)

Mix together all the tartar sauce ingredients. Taste-test and season with salt and pepper if required.

Flounder is a bit on the delicate side, so be gentle when breading, frying, and transporting it from the oil to the plate. You may need a combo of a spatula and a fork to adequately transport the fish.

Use an oil thermometer to take the guesswork out of frying.

The fried flounder can be kept warm in the oven on a baking sheet at 170 to 200°F while frying the remaining batches.

Using the best ingredients, especially seafood, is recommended. I use cod for this particular recipe, but you can use any firm white fish, such as monkfish, snapper, sole, or halibut. Similarly, feel free to mix and match the other seafood ingredients depending on what is freshest. You may want to use lobster instead of shrimp, or all mussels and no clams, for example. Your best bet will be to ask your fishmonger which is freshest and go with that.

It's tempting to want to throw all the seafood in at once to cook, but avoid that, as it will leave you with overcooked ingredients. It's important to begin cooking the seafood requiring the most time first (the squid), followed by the fish, and so on.

Go easy on the salt since the shellfish will have a lot of it. Season with salt and pepper to taste right at the end to get the flavors just right.

SIP & FEAST TIPS

ZUPPA DI PESCE

MAKES: 4–6 SERVINGS • **PREP:** 15 MINUTES • **COOK:** 45 MINUTES

Zuppa di pesce, which translates to "fish soup," will always hold a special place in my memory. Growing up, when my parents would take us to dinner, we'd usually wind up at either at a Chinese or Italian restaurant. If we were eating Italian, I could count on my Irish-French dad ordering the zuppa di pesce. Honestly, I think he ordered it as a way to impress my mom, who's 100% Italian, with his attempt to "speak Italian."

Luckily for my dad, zuppa di pesce was and still is available at nearly every Italian American restaurant on Long Island, and for good reason. It's full of flavor from the fennel, shallots, and wine; the variety of seafood presents texture and depth; and most importantly, it allows my dad to exercise his linguistic skills.

Zuppa di pesce is perfect any time of the year, but it's especially good for Christmas Eve's Feast of the Seven Fishes.

INGREDIENTS

- ¼ cup (60 ml) extra virgin olive oil
- 2 medium shallots, diced
- 1 medium fennel bulb, thinly sliced
- 5 cloves garlic, sliced
- ½ teaspoon crushed hot red pepper flakes, optional
- 1 cup (240 ml) dry white wine
- 2 (28-ounce) cans plum tomatoes, hand crushed or pulsed in a blender
- 1¼ cups (320 ml) clam juice
- ¾ pound (340 g) squid, cleaned, tubes cut into ½-inch rings and large tentacles cut in half
- ¾ pound (340 g) cod, or other meaty white fish like monkfish, striped bass, red snapper, etc.
- 12 littleneck clams or other clams, scrubbed and purged
- 1 pound (454 g) mussels, scrubbed and beards removed
- ¾ pound (340 g) extra-large shrimp, peeled and deveined (26 count)
- Salt and pepper, to taste
- ¼ cup minced flat-leaf Italian parsley
- Fennel fronds, for garnish, optional

INSTRUCTIONS

Heat a large Dutch oven or heavy pot over medium-low heat. Add the olive oil, shallots, and sliced fennel and sauté until softened a bit, about 5 minutes. Then add the garlic and cook for 2 minutes more, until fragrant.

Add the red pepper flakes and cook for 30 seconds, then add the wine and turn the heat to medium-high. Scrape the bottom of the pot with a wooden spoon to dislodge the brown bits. Cook the wine for 90 seconds, then turn the heat to medium and add the tomatoes and clam juice. Cook the sauce at a moderate simmer for 10 minutes before adding any seafood.

Add the squid and cook for 15 minutes so that it begins to soften. Next, add the fish and cook for 5 more minutes, then add the clams and cover with a lid. Cook for 5 to 7 minutes longer or until the clams just start to open.

Finally, add the mussels and shrimp and cover with the lid. Cook until the shrimp are pink and cooked through and the mussels open, 5 to 7 minutes. Any clams or mussels that do not open should be removed and discarded because they were likely dead prior to cooking and therefore are not safe to consume.

Taste-test and add salt and pepper to taste. When satisfied, turn the heat off and add the parsley and fennel fronds, if using. Serve in bowls with toasted Italian bread and drizzled with your best extra virgin olive oil, if desired.

NEW YORK–STYLE EGGPLANT PARM

MAKES: 8–10 SERVINGS • **PREP:** 15 MINUTES • **SALT:** 1 HOUR • **COOK:** 1 HOUR, 30 MINUTES

There are many ways to prepare eggplant parm. The original *parmigiana di melanzane* that hails from Sicily does not include any breading and is big on eggplant flavor, while the Neapolitan version often uses an egg-and-pecorino batter to encase the eggplant slices.

While both versions are great, the New York–style eggplant parm is probably my favorite. It's the eggplant parm that can be found at most Italian American restaurants in the New York metropolitan area, the one used to make eggplant parm heroes at pizzerias, and the one that Tara and I both grew up eating.

This version relies on a flour, egg, and breadcrumb dredging process, followed by frying the eggplant disks until golden. They're topped with a simple marinara sauce and cheese and baked until bubbly and delicious. Serve with a side of pasta and a sautéed green for a complete meal.

FOR THE EGGPLANT

- 3 medium eggplants (2½ to 3 pounds/1.1 to 1.4 kg in all), peeled and sliced into ¼-inch rounds
- Kosher salt (see notes opposite)
- 1½ cups (150 g) Italian seasoned breadcrumbs
- ½ cup (45 g) grated pecorino Romano cheese
- ¼ cup minced flat-leaf Italian parsley
- 1 teaspoon dried oregano
- ½ teaspoon ground black pepper
- 8 large eggs, plus more if needed
- 1 cup (130 g) all-purpose flour, for dredging
- Neutral oil, for frying

FOR THE MARINARA SAUCE

- 3 tablespoons (45 ml) extra virgin olive oil
- 8 cloves garlic, sliced
- ½ teaspoon crushed hot red pepper flakes
- 3 (28-ounce) cans plum tomatoes, hand crushed or pulsed in a blender
- Salt and pepper, to taste
- 3 large basil leaves

SALT THE EGGPLANT

Sprinkle the eggplant slices with salt, then place in a colander with a plate beneath it to drain. Place another plate on top of the eggplant and set a weight on it (a can or two of tomatoes works well) to help remove as much water as possible. Let rest for at least 1 hour, then rinse or thoroughly wipe the pieces with a damp towel to remove most of the excess salt. Pat the pieces dry. They are now ready for frying.

FOR THE MARINARA SAUCE

While the eggplant rests, heat the olive oil in a large pot or saucepan over medium heat and add the garlic.

Cook until the garlic turns golden, stirring occasionally, for 2 to 3 minutes, then add the red pepper flakes and cook for 30 seconds more. Add the tomatoes and bring the sauce to a simmer, stirring occasionally.

Season the sauce with salt and pepper to taste and add the basil leaves. Simmer for 15 minutes, then set the sauce aside and cover to keep warm, or keep warm over very low heat. You will need about 5 cups (1.4 L) of sauce for the eggplant parm; serve the extra with pasta or save for another use.

FOR THE EGGPLANT

In a large bowl mix together the breadcrumbs, pecorino, parsley, oregano, and pepper. In a separate large bowl, beat the eggs. Set up a third large bowl with the flour. Line a baking sheet with parchment paper and set aside.

Pat the eggplant pieces dry, then dredge in the flour and shake off the excess. Place the eggplant into the egg mixture, then let it drain for a few seconds and place into the breadcrumbs to coat on both sides. Place the coated eggplant pieces on the parchment-lined baking sheet.

Meanwhile, fill a large heavy pan or pot with enough neutral oil to at least ½ inch high and heat the oil to 360 to 370°F.

Working in batches, fry the eggplant until golden, about 3 minutes per side, then place on a paper towel–lined plate to drain. Blot the fried eggplant with paper towels to remove excess oil.

The eggplant can be sliced lengthwise if you prefer.

You'll need enough salt to liberally salt the eggplant slices. While the salting step is optional, it is highly recommended. The salt removes excess water from the eggplant, yielding a better fry. Just be sure to remove the salt by rinsing under water or thoroughly wiping with damp towels. Be sure the pieces are completely dry before dredging and frying.

After frying, be sure to let the eggplant drain on paper towels, and blot any excess oil from the eggplant before assembling the parmigiana. This will help prevent an overly oily finished product.

FOR ASSEMBLY

1 pound (454 g) shredded mozzarella cheese

½ cup (45 g) grated pecorino Romano cheese, plus more for serving

¼ cup packed basil leaves, hand torn

FOR ASSEMBLY

Preheat the oven to 350°F and set the rack to the middle level.

Place a thick layer of marinara sauce into a 9-x-13-inch baking dish, then add 1 layer of eggplant. Distributing equally among the layers (you will have anywhere from 3 to 4 layers depending on how thick the eggplant slices are after salting), add more sauce, then some of the shredded mozzarella, grated pecorino, and torn basil leaves. Repeat the layers to the top of the baking dish.

Bake for 35 to 40 minutes. For a browner top, broil for the last 1 to 3 minutes, but watch carefully the whole time.

Let the eggplant parm rest for at least 20 minutes to solidify before serving. Serve with grated cheese and extra sauce.

STUFFED CALAMARI

MAKES: 4–6 SERVINGS • PREP: 20 MINUTES • COOK: 1 HOUR, 10 MINUTES

Stuffed calamari is a delicious dish that's inspired by the flavors of the Mediterranean and very popular for Christmas Eve's Feast of the Seven Fishes.

The squid are stuffed with a flavorful combo of garlic, anchovy, breadcrumbs, and pignoli nuts, then braised until tender in a white wine and tomato sauce. While my stuffing is a simple one, you can certainly add to it. Capers, olives, and raisins are all great additions. You can also use diced shrimp in place of the squid tentacles, if desired.

Stuffed calamari is best served with some crusty bread, but it would also be great with rice.

INGREDIENTS

½ cup (120 ml) extra virgin olive oil, divided

2 anchovy fillets

7 cloves garlic, 2 cloves minced and 5 cloves thinly sliced

1 pound (454 g) squid, cleaned and tentacles minced

¼ cup (35 g) finely chopped pignoli nuts

1 cup (100 g) plain breadcrumbs

½ cup minced flat-leaf Italian parsley

1 teaspoon dried Sicilian oregano

¾ cup (180 ml) dry white wine, divided

½ cup (45 g) grated pecorino Romano cheese

Salt and pepper, to taste

½ teaspoon crushed hot red pepper flakes

2 cups (480 ml) passata (see notes below)

INSTRUCTIONS

Preheat the oven to 350°F and set the rack to the middle level.

Heat ¼ cup of the olive oil in a large pan over medium heat and add the anchovies and 2 cloves of the minced garlic. Break up the anchovies with a wooden spoon and cook until the garlic is fragrant and lightly golden, then add the minced tentacles and cook for 2 to 3 minutes, stirring occasionally. Add the pignoli nuts and cook for another minute.

Add the breadcrumbs, parsley, and oregano and mix to combine. Turn off the heat and mix in ¼ cup of wine and the pecorino. If the stuffing is too dry, add a touch more wine. Taste-test and season with salt and pepper if required. Let the stuffing cool for at least 10 minutes.

Using a pastry bag, stuff each squid tube halfway only so that they don't burst, then use a toothpick to close the ends.

Heat the remaining ¼ cup of olive oil in a large ovenproof pan over medium heat and, once it's shimmering, add the stuffed calamari tubes and sear for roughly 1 minute per side. They will shrink rapidly as they cook. Place the seared calamari onto a plate and cover with tented foil.

Add the sliced garlic to the pan and cook until golden, then add the red pepper flakes and cook for another 30 seconds. Add the remaining ½ cup of wine and the passata and bring to a simmer. Season with salt and pepper to taste, then turn off the heat.

Add the stuffed calamari to the pan and spoon sauce over each one. Cover tightly with foil and place in the oven for 45 minutes, then check for tenderness. If the calamari are still tough (larger tubes might be), return to the oven and check again after 20 minutes.

Serve the stuffed calamari with crusty bread to mop up the sauce, if desired.

I use passata, a tomato puree that's strained to remove the seeds and skin, because I prefer a smoother texture for this particular sauce. But you can use crushed tomatoes if you can't find passata.

Using a pastry bag for the stuffing is recommended, as it will make the process so much easier. When stuffing, be sure to fill the tubes halfway or very lightly, they will shrink when cooked and could burst.

The larger the squid tubes, the longer they will take to braise and become tender.

THE SAVVY HOST'S LESS-STRESS DINNER PARTY

The key to hosting a successful and low-stress dinner party lies in the prep. I'm a firm believer that happy hosts yield joyful guests, and having hosted many gatherings, Tara and I can safely say that the more you can do ahead of your guests' arrival, the happier you'll be.

Selecting a theme focused on a specific region or country's cuisine can also be a fun way to get your guests excited and engaged in the planning process. For example, invite your guests to an Italian- or French-inspired dinner party and ask that they bring wine, cheese, or desserts that represent those regions. Then use one of the following sample menus for your party.

MENU #1 (Italian-Inspired)

SPIEDINI ALLA ROMANA (page 33) and **EGGPLANT CAPONATA** (make ahead; page 26)

PAPPARDELLE WITH BRAISED SHORT RIB RAGU (make the ragu ahead, then boil your pasta right before eating and toss with the ragu; page 86)

SICILIAN FENNEL AND ORANGE SALAD (make ahead; page 195)

MENU #2 (Italian-Inspired)

THE EASIEST CANNELLINI DIP (make ahead; page 25) with vegetable crudités and **TUSCAN-STYLE BALSAMIC-GLAZED RIBS** (make ahead; page 138)

TUSCAN WHITE BEAN SOUP (make ahead; page 164)

PEPOSO (make ahead; page 175) with **CREAMY POLENTA** (page 105) or crusty bread and **ROASTED ASPARAGUS WITH LEMON AND PARMESAN** (make ahead; page 49)

MENU #3 (French-Inspired)

TOMATO CONFIT (make a few hours before guests arrive and serve warm; page 50), with crusty bread, cheese, fresh grapes, and **ANTIPASTO** (see page 52)

FRENCH ONION SOUP (make ahead and warm in crocks with bread and cheese before serving; page 185)

BEEF BOURGUIGNON (make ahead, but keep the mushrooms and pearl onions separate and plate right before serving; page 176), serve with baguette or mashed potatoes

DESSERTS

Feel free to enlist the help of your guests when it comes to the drinks and desserts! Letting them know you're having a theme can help them decide what to bring. For example, if you're going with the French-inspired menu, your guests may wish to stay on theme and bring some French pastries.

If you prefer to make dessert yourself, any of these recipes would be great for a dinner party and all can be made ahead with relative ease.

TIRAMISU (page 209)

PANNA COTTA WITH FRESH BERRIES (page 210)

FLOURLESS CHOCOLATE CAKE (page 218)

GRAPEFRUIT OLIVE OIL CAKE (page 217)

SOUPS and STEWS

There's nothing like walking through your front door and being welcomed by the smell of soup or stew simmering on the stove. As a kid, I could always tell what soup was being made just by its aroma, and now that I'm the parent, I adore the fact that my kids can do the same when they get home from school.

To me, soups and stews are some of the most personal dishes you can make, meaning they're meals that we, as the cooks, get to pour our love into. We may make soup as a gesture to help a loved one feel better, or to welcome and celebrate cooler weather and shorter days, or simply because we love the end result of a warm and intensely flavorful and satisfying meal.

And speaking of flavor, many of these soups and stews (and the chili!) are even better when eaten the next day. Giving them some time to hang out in the fridge allows the flavors to further develop and intensify.

FRAN'S PASTA E FAGIOLI

MAKES: 6–8 SERVINGS • **PREP:** 5 MINUTES • **COOK:** 35 MINUTES

Almost everyone's Italian American mom, nonna, or poppa has their own version of pasta fagioli ("pasta fazool"). The version that's available on my website is my own. It contains only three plum tomatoes, making it almost white, and a rosemary sprig. The version you see here in this cookbook is my mom's version. It runs more toward the red end of the spectrum, using a whole 14-ounce can of plum tomatoes, sans rosemary.

When I first thought about writing this book, this was one recipe I knew for sure I wanted to add. I love that when compared to my version, it demonstrates the diversity in this dish. It's proof that there's more than one way to make a classic, and that recipes can evolve, even within the same family.

I recommend serving with crusty bread, grated cheese, hot red pepper flakes, or black pepper on the side and a drizzle of some high-quality extra virgin olive oil.

Pasta fagioli is hearty enough to be served as a meal alongside a salad.

INGREDIENTS

⅓ cup (80 ml) extra virgin olive oil

1 medium onion, diced

10 cloves garlic, roughly chopped

½ teaspoon crushed hot red pepper flakes

6 cups (1.4 L) water, plus more as needed

1 (14-ounce) can plum tomatoes, hand crushed or pulsed in a blender

2 teaspoons kosher salt, plus more to taste

3 (16-ounce) cans cannellini beans, drained but not rinsed

2 cups (260 g) ditalini, or small shells or elbows

Black pepper, to taste

INSTRUCTIONS

Heat the olive oil in a large pot over medium heat. Add the onion and a pinch of salt and cook until soft and translucent, 5 to 7 minutes, stirring occasionally.

Add the garlic and cook for 3 to 4 minutes more or until very golden. Add the red pepper flakes and cook for 30 seconds.

Next, add the water, tomatoes, and salt and give it a stir. Add the beans and bring to a boil for 5 minutes.

Lower the heat back to medium and crush some of the beans by smashing them against the side of the pot with a wooden spoon.

Add the pasta and cook until al dente. Keep an eye on the pot and stir frequently to avoid sticking. The pasta will absorb much of the liquid, so add more water as needed. The final consistency of the pasta fagioli is 100% a personal preference. If you like it soupier, add more water.

Once the pasta is al dente, turn off the heat and taste-test. Add black pepper to taste and adjust the salt and red pepper flakes as needed.

When satisfied with the taste, serve in bowls and enjoy.

Pasta shapes like ditalini, small shells, elbows, and farfalline are all great choices. Even broken spaghetti works.

If you plan to have leftovers, be sure to cook and store the pasta separately. Otherwise, it's better to cook the pasta in the sauce to better absorb the flavors.

TUSCAN WHITE BEAN SOUP

MAKES: 6–8 SERVINGS • **PREP:** 10 MINUTES • **ROAST:** 50 MINUTES • **COOK:** 55 MINUTES

Tuscan white bean soup may be one of the easiest soups you can make. We love it because it is nourishing, filling, and completely budget-friendly. It's also customizable, so if you want to make it vegetarian or vegan you can do that by omitting the chicken stock, pancetta, and Parmigiano-Reggiano rind and replacing the chicken stock with vegetable stock or water. It will still have incredible flavor, thanks to the roasted garlic!

Depending on my mood when I'm making this, I'll sometimes leave the beans intact, or I'll use an immersion blender to make a thicker, creamier soup. Both ways are good!

This soup is great as a precursor to a larger meal, but it is bold enough to shine by itself, or alongside a salad or sandwich. I suggest serving it with a drizzle of extra virgin olive oil, grated parmesan, and crusty bread on the side.

FOR THE ROASTED GARLIC

1 head garlic

Extra virgin olive oil

FOR THE SOUP

¼ cup (60 ml) extra virgin olive oil

¼ pound (113 g) pancetta, diced

4 celery ribs, diced

3 medium carrots, diced

1 large onion, diced

Salt and pepper, to taste

¼ teaspoon crushed hot red pepper flakes

6 cups (1.5 L) low-sodium chicken stock, plus more as needed

3 (16-ounce) cans cannellini beans, drained but not rinsed

1 small Parmigiano-Reggiano cheese rind, optional

3 sprigs rosemary or thyme

1 large bay leaf

FOR THE ROASTED GARLIC

Preheat the oven to 400°F and cut off the top ¼ inch of the garlic head, exposing the tops of the cloves. Place the head cut side up on a sheet of foil and drizzle with a bit of olive oil. Wrap tightly with the foil and place onto a baking sheet. Bake for 40 to 50 minutes or until golden and soft. Remove the cloves from the skin by squeezing them out and set aside for the soup.

FOR THE SOUP

Meanwhile, heat the olive oil in a large heavy pot over a touch less than medium heat. Sauté the pancetta until most of the fat renders, about 10 minutes. Add the celery, carrots, onion, and a pinch of salt and continue to cook, stirring occasionally, for 10 more minutes or until the veggies are softened.

Add the red pepper flakes and cook for 30 seconds, then add the roasted garlic cloves, chicken stock, beans, cheese rind, if using, rosemary, and bay leaf. Bring to a boil, then lower to a simmer and cook for 15 to 20 minutes.

Mash some of the beans with a wooden spoon against the side of the pot to help thicken the soup. For a thicker soup use an immersion blender, making sure to remove the parm rind, rosemary stems, and bay leaf before blending.

Taste the soup and add salt and pepper to taste. Remove the cheese rind, rosemary stems, and bay leaf before serving. If the soup is too thick, thin it with a bit more stock or water. Serve in bowls and enjoy.

SIP & FEAST TIPS

Roasted garlic can be prepped in advance and stored in the refrigerator for up to 1 week. You may also be able to find roasted garlic cloves at the olive bar section of your grocery store.

You can use dried beans instead of canned if you like—just be sure to soak them overnight to soften and note that the cooking time may increase.

ESCAROLE AND BEAN SOUP

MAKES: 6–8 SERVINGS • PREP: 10 MINUTES • COOK: 45 MINUTES

Escarole and bean soup is nourishing, comforting, and can be ready in less than an hour. Pancetta, onion, garlic, and cannellini beans are simmered with potatoes and escarole in a tasty broth. This is yet another recipe I grew up eating, and every time I make it now, I wonder why I don't make it more often!

This soup is best served with a side of crusty bread, a drizzle of extra virgin olive oil, and plenty of Parmigiano-Reggiano or pecorino Romano cheese.

INGREDIENTS

- ¼ cup (60 ml) extra virgin olive oil
- ¼ pound (113 g) pancetta, diced
- 3 celery ribs, diced
- 1 medium onion, diced
- 2 medium Russet potatoes, peeled and cut into small cubes
- 3 cloves garlic, sliced
- 6 cups (1.5 L) low-sodium chicken stock, plus more as needed
- 3 (16-ounce) cans cannellini beans, drained but not rinsed
- 1 small Parmigiano-Reggiano cheese rind, optional
- 1 head escarole, washed and chopped
- Salt and pepper, to taste
- ½ cup (45 grams) grated Parmigiano-Reggiano cheese, for serving

INSTRUCTIONS

Heat the olive oil in a large heavy pot over medium-low heat. Add the pancetta and sauté until most of the fat renders, about 10 minutes, then add the celery, onion, and a pinch of salt and continue to cook, stirring occasionally, for 7 to 10 minutes or until the veggies are softened.

Add the potatoes and cook for 5 minutes, stirring frequently to coat with the oil.

Add the garlic and cook for 2 minutes, then add the chicken stock, beans, and cheese rind, if using. Bring to a boil, then lower to a simmer. Let the soup simmer for 15 to 20 minutes or until the potatoes and beans are tender.

Using a wooden spoon, mash some of the beans and potatoes against the side of the pot to help thicken the soup. Add the escarole and cook until tender, 5 to 7 minutes or longer depending on how tender you want it. Once tender, season with salt and pepper to taste. If the soup is too thick, add more chicken stock or water to thin it to the desired consistency.

Remove the cheese rind and serve in bowls with grated cheese on top.

The outer leaves and the core of the escarole should be discarded. To clean and remove the grit from the escarole, use a large salad spinner or soak the leaves in a large bowl with cold water for 5 minutes, then remove and change the water 1 to 2 more times.

For a vegetarian soup, omit the pancetta and use vegetable stock in place of chicken stock.

ITALIAN LENTIL SOUP

MAKES: 6–8 SERVINGS • **PREP:** 10 MINUTES • **COOK:** 1 HOUR

One of the things I like best about Italian lentil soup is that it can be made with items that I almost always have in the pantry and the refrigerator. I usually keep several bags of lentils on hand, as well as canned plum tomatoes. Carrots, celery, and onions are also always in my kitchen waiting to be used in some way.

I also appreciate the simplicity of Italian lentil soup. This is the lentil soup I grew up eating, and there's nothing fancy about it at all. In fact, it is really basic, in the best way possible.

Feel free to add toppings to yours as well. My go-to is grated cheese and a drizzle of extra virgin olive oil, James and Sammy love red wine vinegar on theirs, and Tara always adds a scoop of Greek yogurt to hers. Lentil soup is great alongside a salad, sandwich, or some crusty bread.

INGREDIENTS

¼ cup (60 ml) extra virgin olive oil

1 medium onion, diced

2 celery ribs, diced

2 medium carrots, diced

Salt and pepper, to taste

⅓ cup (85 g) tomato paste

1 pound (454 g) brown or green lentils (see notes below)

1 cup (240 ml) crushed plum tomatoes

1 small Parmigiano-Reggiano cheese rind, optional

1 teaspoon dried oregano

8 cups (1.9 L) water

½ pound (226 g) baby spinach

INSTRUCTIONS

Heat a large heavy pot over medium-low heat and add the olive oil, onion, celery, carrots, and a pinch of salt. Cook, stirring occasionally, until soft and translucent, about 10 minutes.

Add the tomato paste and cook, stirring frequently, for 5 minutes, then add the lentils, plum tomatoes, cheese rind, if using, oregano, and water. Bring to a boil, then lower the heat and cook at a simmer until the lentils are soft, 45 to 50 minutes.

After the lentils are cooked through and tender, turn off the heat and add the spinach.

Taste-test and add salt and pepper to taste and serve.

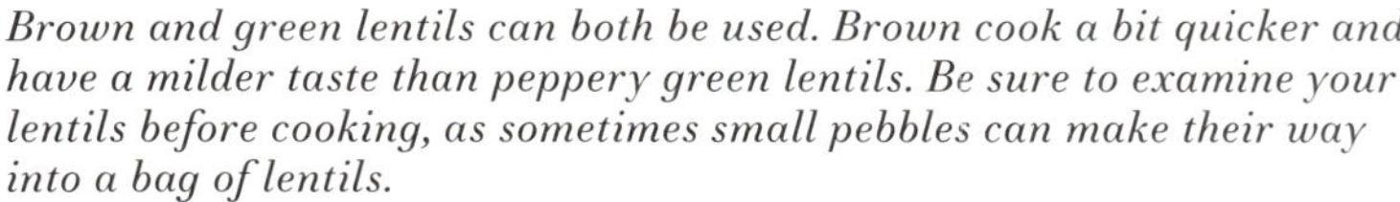

Brown and green lentils can both be used. Brown cook a bit quicker and have a milder taste than peppery green lentils. Be sure to examine your lentils before cooking, as sometimes small pebbles can make their way into a bag of lentils.

For even more flavor, feel free to add a ham hock to the soup. It can be added at the same time as the lentils.

ITALIAN ZUCCHINI AND BROKEN SPAGHETTI SOUP

MAKES: 6–8 SERVINGS • **PREP:** 5 MINUTES • **COOK:** 25 MINUTES

Italian zucchini soup with broken spaghetti is truly a nostalgia-evoking dish for me. To this day I can still hear the sound of my grandma breaking the spaghetti in her kitchen as she'd prepare to make this soup with the zucchini from our garden.

Similar to other soups in this cookbook, this one is economical and founded on the "waste not, want not" mentality that was so prevalent among first- and second-generation Italian Americans during the early 1900s. This recipe is a modern and more accessible interpretation of *cucuzza e tenerumi* soup (see the notes below for more information).

Years later, this is still a favorite soup of mine because it's cheap (especially if you grow your own zucchini) and so simple that it can be made in under 30 minutes—proof that even the simplest of recipes can transcend generations. Serve alongside a salad or sandwich for a full meal or on its own with some grated pecorino, a drizzle of extra virgin olive oil, and crusty Italian bread on the side.

INGREDIENTS

⅓ cup (80 ml) extra virgin olive oil, plus more for serving

1 medium onion, diced

Salt and pepper, to taste

6 cloves garlic, chopped

½ teaspoon crushed hot red pepper flakes, optional

4 to 5 medium zucchini, cubed, or cucuzza (see notes below)

1 (14-ounce) can plum tomatoes, hand crushed or pulsed in a blender (see notes below)

6 cups (1.5 L) water

½ pound (226 g) spaghetti, broken into bite-sized pieces

¼ cup packed chopped basil

¼ cup packed chopped flat-leaf Italian parsley

Grated pecorino Romano cheese, for serving

INSTRUCTIONS

Bring a large pot of salted water to boil.

Heat a separate large pot over medium-low heat and add the olive oil, onion, and a pinch of salt. Sauté for 5 to 7 minutes or until soft, then add the garlic and cook for 1 to 2 minutes longer or until lightly golden and fragrant.

Add the red pepper flakes and cook for 30 seconds more, then add the zucchini. Turn the heat to medium and sauté the zucchini for about 10 minutes or until fairly soft.

Add the tomatoes to the pot and continue to cook for a few minutes. Season with salt and pepper, then add the water and bring the soup to a simmer.

Meanwhile, cook the spaghetti in the salted boiling water until al dente.

Once the soup is simmering, taste-test and season with more salt and pepper if necessary. Once satisfied, turn off the heat and add the al dente spaghetti, basil, and parsley. Mix together.

If the soup is too thick, add a bit more water. Serve the soup in bowls topped with grated cheese, and enjoy.

SIP & FEAST TIPS

You can also use 3 to 4 fresh plum tomatoes that have been blanched to remove their skins in place of the canned plum tomatoes.

Many Italian American gardeners grow snake zucchini or cucuzza *(slang "gagootz"). Cucuzza is a gourd that grows massively and rewards its grower with a bountiful harvest of squash and leaves. They are typically grown on a large hanging wood trellis and can often grow to 4 feet or larger. The leaves of the cucuzza, also known as* tenerumi, *are often chopped up and added to the zucchini soup. If you grow cucuzza, definitely use those leaves!*

ITALIAN BEEF SOUP

MAKES: 6–8 SERVINGS • **PREP:** 5 MINUTES • **COOK:** AT LEAST 3 HOURS, 30 MINUTES

When it comes to childhood memories, this Italian beef soup packs a punch for me! This is a soup my mom would make often, and it always tasted extra good when I was sick or just not feeling well. The beef *brodo*, or broth, is warm and nourishing and the tender beef and carrots are tasty and easy to eat.

This is a great one to make ahead and save in the freezer for whenever you need a little extra TLC.

INGREDIENTS

¼ cup (60 ml) extra virgin olive oil

3 pounds (1.4 kg) chuck roast

1 tablespoon (10 g) kosher salt, plus more to taste

1 teaspoon ground black pepper, plus more to taste

5 large carrots, cut in half

3 celery ribs with leaves, cut in half

1 large white onion, cut in half

6 cups (1.5 L) water

4 cups (1 L) no-sodium beef stock

1 (14-ounce) can whole plum tomatoes

¼ cup packed flat-leaf Italian parsley leaves and stems

10 black peppercorns

2 large bay leaves

3 whole cloves

1 pound (454 g) farfalline, or ditalini, or small shells

Grated pecorino Romano cheese, for serving

INSTRUCTIONS

Heat the olive oil in a large pot over medium heat. Pat the chuck roast very dry with paper towels and season with the salt and ground black pepper. Sear the roast in the pot on all sides until well browned, 10 to 15 minutes total. Remove the roast and set on a plate.

Add the carrots, celery, onion, a splash of water, and a pinch of salt to the same pot. With a wooden spoon, scrape the bottom of the pot to dislodge any brown bits. Sauté the vegetables for 10 minutes.

Add the water, beef stock, tomatoes, parsley, peppercorns, bay leaves, and cloves to the pot and bring to a boil.

Once boiling, use a large flat spoon to skim any scum off the top. Lower the heat, add the chuck roast back to the pot, and place a lid on the pot, leaving it slightly cracked. Simmer over low heat for 3 to 4 hours or until the beef is very tender. Every 25 to 30 minutes, skim the scum off the top and discard it. Do not stir it, since that will make the broth cloudy.

Once the beef is tender, remove and set it on a plate. Strain the brodo by gently ladling it through a fine-mesh sieve placed over another large pot. Ladling the brodo instead of pouring it helps keep it clear. Discard all of the veggies except for the carrots.

The fat will rise to the top of the brodo. Remove the fat with a ladle, a ladle with ice cubes, a fat separator, or paper towels. Or you can make the brodo up to this point the day before and store it in the fridge overnight; the fat will rise to the top and can be easily removed.

Shred the beef and chop the carrots. Taste-test and season with salt and pepper if required. Bring a pot of salted water to boil and cook the pasta to al dente.

Serve the soup in bowls with a bit of pasta and shredded beef, a few of the carrots, and plenty of pecorino in each bowl.

It is recommended to keep the pasta separate so it does not become overly soft. Add the amount you'd like to your bowl before ladling the soup.

You can add the shredded beef back to the pot if you'd like, but be aware that it may cloud the soup. Some folks prefer a very clear brodo, but if that's not important to you, then add it.

PEPOSO

MAKES: 4 SERVINGS • **PREP:** 5 MINUTES • **COOK:** 3 HOURS

The first time I ever made peposo, I was blown away by the incredible flavor and the fact that making it requires just a handful of ingredients.

This Tuscan-style black pepper stew is a favorite in our home and among our readers. We make it often, especially in the cooler months, and while it's traditionally served with crusty bread, I especially love it over Creamy Polenta (page 105).

And no need to look twice, the 1½ tablespoons of black peppercorns is correct. Trust the recipe, and revel in the delicious results!

INGREDIENTS

2½ pounds (1.2 kg) chuck roast, cut into chunks

2 teaspoons kosher salt

3 tablespoons (45 ml) extra virgin olive oil

8 cloves garlic

1½ tablespoons (12 g) black peppercorns, crushed with a mallet

1 (750 ml) bottle Chianti or other dry red wine

INSTRUCTIONS

Using paper towels, pat the beef chunks very dry and season them with the salt on all sides.

Heat a large Dutch oven over medium heat, add the olive oil and garlic, and cook for 1 to 2 minutes, or until the cloves turn lightly golden. Remove the garlic cloves and set aside for later.

Working in batches to avoid crowding the pan, add the beef chunks and sear on all sides, 5 to 6 minutes total per batch, then place the beef on a plate.

Add the black pepper to the oil and cook for 30 seconds. Turn the heat up to medium-high and add the red wine. Once bubbling, use a wooden spoon to gently dislodge the brown bits from the bottom of the pot. Let the wine bubble for 2 to 3 minutes, then turn the heat down to medium-low.

Return the seared beef and garlic cloves to the pot, give it a stir, and cover with a lid. Cook for 1½ hours, then remove the lid and continue to cook for another 1 to 1½ hours or until tender. Make sure to stir the meat every so often and to check for tenderness. The meat should be tender but not falling apart.

Once the meat is tender, you can remove it to a plate and reduce the liquid in the pot by bringing it to a boil. If the liquid is already thick enough, skip the boiling step and serve immediately.

If too much evaporation occurs, simply add a ½ cup or so of water to the pot and make sure that the heat is set to low.

Since pepper is one of the main ingredients in peposo, it's imperative to use freshly crushed pepper. A meat mallet works well to crush the whole black peppercorns, or the coarse grind setting on a pepper mill also works.

A Super Tuscan or Chianti would work well for this recipe, but you can also use a Cabernet Sauvignon.

Chuck roast is inherently fatty, so if you'd like to remove some of the fat from the dish, you can do so by trimming the chuck before you sear it, or skimming the fat from the top of the peposo with a slotted spoon.

SIP & FEAST TIPS

BEEF BOURGUIGNON

MAKES: 6–8 SERVINGS • PREP: 15 MINUTES • COOK: 3 HOURS, 30 MINUTES

We could not write this book without including beef bourguignon. It's Tara's favorite dish of all, and one whose technique I seemed to have mastered in recent years. It's a dish I grew up watching Julia Child make, and learning to make it myself has made me a better cook.

Often regarded as the king of all beef dishes, this comforting French-style beef stew combines tender chunks of beef braised in red wine with carrots, herbs, and sautéed pearl onions and mushrooms. While you can cook the pearl onions and mushrooms along with the stew, the traditional way is to cook these ingredients separately and add them at the end to finish the dish. We will often save these on the side and top each plate with a few mushrooms and onions to ensure everyone gets an even amount.

Serve beef bourguignon with a chunk of crusty bread or mashed or roasted potatoes. And because it's even *better* the next day, it's the perfect dinner party main course (see pages 158–159).

FOR THE STEW

- ½ pound (226 g) thick-cut bacon, cut into ¼-inch pieces
- 3 pounds (1.4 kg) beef chuck, trimmed of fat and cut into 2-inch cubes
- Salt and pepper, to taste
- ½ cup (65 g) all-purpose flour
- 1 large white onion, chopped
- 2 large carrots, cut into 2-inch chunks
- 6 cloves garlic, minced
- ¼ cup (60 g) tomato paste
- 3 cups (720 ml) Burgundy wine, or other dry red wine
- 3 cups (720 ml) low-sodium beef broth or stock
- 8 sprigs thyme, tied together
- 2 large bay leaves

FOR THE STEW

Preheat the oven to 350°F and set the rack to the middle level with enough room to accommodate a large Dutch oven and its lid.

Heat a large Dutch oven over medium heat and add the bacon. Cook, stirring occasionally, until most of the fat has rendered, 7 to 10 minutes, then remove the bacon with a slotted spoon and set on a paper towel–lined plate to drain, leaving the fat in the pot.

Pat the beef cubes very dry with paper towels, then season with salt and pepper. Toss the beef cubes with the flour, then shake off the excess and save the extra flour for later in the recipe. Working in batches if necessary, sear the beef until well browned on all sides, 5 to 7 minutes per batch. Place the beef onto another plate and set aside.

Remove the excess bacon and beef fat from the pot, leaving approximately ¼ cup in the pot. Add the onion and cook, stirring occasionally, for 3 to 5 minutes or until slightly softened, then add the carrots and continue to cook until they get a bit of color, 5 to 7 minutes.

Add the garlic to the pot and cook until fragrant, 1 to 2 minutes, then add the tomato paste and cook for another 3 to 4 minutes, stirring frequently to avoid burning. If it starts to burn, just add a couple of ounces of water to the pot to lower the temperature.

Add all of the remaining flour to the pot and use a nylon whisk or wooden spoon to incorporate. Cook until the flour is no longer white, about 2 minutes.

Slowly add the wine and beef broth to the pot while whisking to avoid any lumps. Using a flat wooden spoon, scrape the bottom of the pot to dislodge the brown bits. Add the beef, bacon, thyme, and bay leaves to the pot and turn off the heat.

Cover the pot and place it in the oven to cook for 2½ to 3 hours or until the beef is very tender. *Note:* Check on the beef at the 90-minute mark. If the sauce is too thick and sticking to the bottom of the pot, add ½ cup of water and mix well before returning the pot back to the oven.

CONTINUED

BEEF BOURGUIGNON (CONTINUED)

FOR FINISHING

Salt and pepper, to taste

2 tablespoons (30 ml) extra virgin olive oil

16 pearl onions

1 pound (454 g) cremini mushrooms, quartered

4 tablespoons (56 g) butter

2 teaspoons thyme leaves

3 tablespoons minced flat-leaf Italian parsley

FOR FINISHING

Once the beef is tender, remove the pot from the oven, taste-test, and season with salt and pepper, if required. Discard the bay leaves and thyme. Use a spoon to skim any visible fat from the top.

If the sauce is too thin, strain it into another pot, separating the liquid from the other ingredients. Place the pot over medium-high heat and cook until the sauce coats the back of a wooden spoon, then combine the sauce and the other ingredients back together. Make sure to keep the pot covered while moving on to the final step below.

Heat a large pan over a touch higher than medium heat. Add the olive oil and the pearl onions and cook until the onions are tender and golden, 4 to 5 minutes, then remove with a slotted spoon, place on a plate, and cover with foil.

Add the mushrooms to the same pan and cook until they release their water and start to brown, 5 to 8 minutes. Once they begin to brown, add the butter and cook until they are glistening, 2 to 3 minutes. Return the pearl onions back to the pan and toss to coat. Turn off the heat and season with salt and pepper and the thyme.

Mix the parsley into the pot with the beef. You can mix all the mushrooms and pearl onions into the pot before, or divide them onto plates so that each person gets a few pearl onions and mushrooms.

This recipe calls for a whole chuck roast, but you can use other cuts of beef such as brisket or top, eye, or bottom round.

Beef bourguignon is traditionally made with red Burgundy wine, which is made from pinot noir grapes in the Burgundy region of France. If you're a stickler for tradition, you can use a French Burgundy, but you'll still get great results using a domestic pinot noir.

If possible, it's best to make this a day ahead, then let the pot cool and refrigerate the stew overnight. The flavors will be more concentrated and the taste will be even better. To reheat the next day, simply simmer on the stovetop over medium-low to medium heat until it's warmed through. You can add a little water to loosen it up if the sauce is too thick.

SIP & FEAST TIPS

BEEF BARLEY SOUP

MAKES: 6–8 SERVINGS • PREP: 5 MINUTES • COOK: 2 HOURS

Calling beef barley soup a soup may be a misnomer. This soup is almost more like a beef stew, since it's incredibly hearty and loaded with stick-to-your-ribs goodness. My recipe includes beef chuck that's braised in broth and red wine along with carrots, celery, onion, and garlic. While the soup takes almost two hours to cook, it's more than worth the wait.

And if you can wait even longer, beef barley soup, like most soups, will taste better the next day. We usually serve this soup with a chunk of crusty bread or garlic bread and a simple green salad.

INGREDIENTS

- 3 tablespoons (45 ml) extra virgin olive oil
- 2 pounds (908 g) beef chuck, cubed
- Salt and pepper, to taste
- 1 medium onion, diced
- 2 celery ribs, diced
- 4 medium carrots, diced
- 3 cloves garlic, minced
- ¾ cup (180 ml) dry red wine
- 6 cups (1.5 L) low-sodium beef broth
- 1 tablespoon (15 ml) Worcestershire sauce
- 3 sprigs thyme
- 1 cup (200 g) pearled barley
- ¼ cup minced flat-leaf Italian parsley

INSTRUCTIONS

Heat a large heavy pot over medium heat and add the olive oil. Pat the beef dry with paper towels and season with the salt and pepper on all sides. Working in batches if required to avoid overcrowding the pot, sear the beef on all sides until well browned, 7 to 10 minutes. Transfer the beef to a plate and set aside.

Add the onion, celery, and carrots to the same pot. Sauté for 5 minutes, then add the garlic and cook for 1 minute longer.

Add the wine and turn the heat to high. Reduce by half, about 2 minutes, and scrape the bottom of the pot with a wooden spoon to dislodge any brown bits.

Add the beef broth, Worcestershire sauce, and thyme, then add the beef back to the pot. Once boiling, turn the heat down to a simmer, partially cover, and cook for 45 minutes.

Add the barley and continue to cook at a simmer until tender, 45 to 60 minutes more. Taste along the way and once the barley is tender, remove the pot from the heat.

Taste again and adjust the salt and pepper to taste. If the soup is too thick, add water or extra low-sodium beef broth to thin it to your preference. Add the parsley right before serving.

It's important to pat the beef cubes dry with paper towels and season them right before you sear them. Seasoning the beef on all sides with salt and pepper will help better flavor the soup.

Barley takes a long time to cook, so be patient. Taste the soup along the way and you'll know it's done when the barley is nice and tender. Regardless of what the bag says, even pearled barley will take 45 to 60 minutes to cook when added to a soup.

SIP & FEAST TIPS

ITALIAN WEDDING SOUP

MAKES: 6–8 SERVINGS • **PREP:** 30 MINUTES • **COOK:** 40 MINUTES

Italian wedding soup is a meal we had frequently when I was growing up, and it never disappointed! This family-friendly meal features tender tiny meatballs and lots of fresh vegetables, like carrots, celery, onion, and escarole. The tiny pearl-shaped pasta, acini di pepe, used for traditional Italian wedding soup rounds out the dish, making this a complete meal.

Rolling out the tiny meatballs can take some time. If you can, ask a friend or loved one to help you with this. It's a great way to bond over food!

I recommend serving the soup with some grated Parmigiano-Reggiano and a drizzle of good extra virgin olive oil.

FOR THE MEATBALLS

¾ cup (75 g) plain breadcrumbs

⅓ cup (90 ml) whole milk

¾ pound (340 g) ground chuck

¾ pound (340 g) ground pork

½ cup (45 g) grated pecorino Romano cheese

¼ cup minced flat-leaf Italian parsley

2 large eggs

3 cloves garlic, finely minced and mashed into a paste

1 teaspoon kosher salt

½ teaspoon ground black pepper

FOR THE SOUP

¼ cup (60 ml) extra virgin olive oil

1 medium onion, diced

2 medium carrots, diced

2 large celery ribs, diced

Salt and pepper, to taste

1 head of escarole, washed and chopped, or 1 pound (454 g) baby spinach

10 cups (2.4 L) low-sodium chicken stock or water, plus more as needed

1 small Parmigiano-Reggiano cheese rind, optional

½ pound (226 g) acini di pepe

FOR THE MEATBALLS

In a large mixing bowl, combine the breadcrumbs and milk and let sit for 5 minutes, then add the remaining meatball ingredients to the bowl and mix to incorporate.

Line a baking sheet with parchment paper. Form very small meatballs (½ inch diameter or less) and place them onto the parchment-lined baking sheet. Place the baking sheet into the fridge and begin making the soup.

FOR THE SOUP

Heat the olive oil in a large pot over medium heat, then add the onion, carrots, celery, and a pinch of salt. Sauté until soft, 7 to 10 minutes, then add the escarole and continue to cook for another 3 minutes. *Note:* If subbing spinach, wait to add it to the soup until after adding the pasta.

Add the chicken stock and the cheese rind, if using, to the pot and bring to a boil. Once boiling, turn the heat down and simmer uncovered for 10 to 15 minutes.

Add the meatballs and simmer for 3 minutes, then add the pasta and continue to cook until al dente. (If using spinach in place of the escarole, add it during the last few minutes of cooking.) Once the pasta has reached al dente, remove the pot from the heat.

Taste the soup and adjust the salt and pepper as needed. Serve with grated cheese and a drizzle of extra virgin olive oil.

Some folks prefer to cook their acini di pepe pasta separately if they intend on serving the soup the next day, to prevent the pasta from becoming too soft. Use your judgment here and do what works best for you.

If you desire a clear broth, do not add the parmesan rind, and precook the meatballs in a separate pot of water, then drain and add them to the soup at the very end. This will prevent much of the fat from clouding the soup. In my opinion, though, it's much better with the parmesan rind and the additional fat.

SIP & FEAST TIPS

This soup, like all soups and stews, tastes much better the next day. I recommend making it one day in advance and letting it sit in the fridge overnight before broiling in soup crocks with the bread and cheese.

French onion soup is very easy to make, but it does require patience and time during the caramelization process. While it doesn't require the continuous stirring of a gumbo roux, it does require a good amount of stirring, and for that reason, it needs to be monitored. If the onions begin to cook too quickly or start to burn, simply add a splash of water (this will bring down the pot temperature) and/or reduce the heat. Do this the whole time while cooking the onions.

SIP & FEAST TIPS

FRENCH ONION SOUP

MAKES: 6 SERVINGS • PREP: 20 MINUTES • COOK: 1 HOUR, 50 MINUTES

French onion soup, when properly made, can be a thing of beauty. With its caramelized onions, vermouth, and beef stock combo, this soup is rich with flavor, and when topped with baguette slices and Gruyère, it's even better.

While French onion soup is widely available in restaurants, there is nothing better than the homemade version. Since the soup itself can be made ahead of time (it's way better made a day in advance), it's a great option for dinner parties. Simply add the bread and cheese, broil, and garnish with fresh thyme before serving.

FOR THE CARAMELIZED ONIONS

2 tablespoons (30 ml) extra virgin olive oil

4 pounds (1.8 kg) yellow onions, sliced thinly from root to stem

⅓ cup (90 ml) water

1 teaspoon kosher salt

4 tablespoons (56 g) butter

FOR THE SOUP

4 cloves garlic, minced

1 tablespoon (15 g) tomato paste

1 tablespoon (8 g) all-purpose flour

½ cup (120 ml) dry vermouth or 1 cup (240 ml) dry white wine

8 cups (1.9 L) low-sodium beef stock

1 tablespoon thyme leaves, plus more for serving

Salt and pepper, to taste

1 tablespoon (15 ml) brandy or sherry, optional

12 (½-inch-thick) slices baguette, or enough to mostly cover 6 soup bowls

1½ cups (170 g) sliced or shredded Gruyère cheese

FOR THE CARAMELIZED ONIONS

Heat the olive oil in a large Dutch oven or heavy pot over medium heat. Add the onions, water, and salt and mix to coat. Cover with the lid and cook for 15 minutes.

Remove the lid, add the butter, and continue to cook, stirring occasionally. Keep an eye on the onions and adjust the heat as needed to avoid burning. Add a splash of water every so often to avoid burning, if necessary. Cook for 60 to 90 minutes longer, until the onions are fully caramelized and have become deep brown and sweet.

FOR THE SOUP

Once the onions are deeply caramelized, add the garlic and cook for 1 to 2 minutes or until fragrant. Add the tomato paste and cook, stirring frequently, for 5 minutes. If the paste begins to burn, just add a splash of water.

Add the flour to the pot and cook, stirring continuously, for 2 minutes or until all of the flour is no longer white.

Add the vermouth and bring to a boil while scraping the bottom of the pan with a wooden spoon to dislodge all of the brown bits.

Once boiling, add the beef stock and thyme and bring to a simmer. Cook at a simmer for at least 20 minutes.

Taste-test and adjust the salt and pepper to taste. Add the brandy or sherry, if using, and stir to combine. At this point, the soup is done and can be placed into crocks for serving or stored overnight for even more flavor.

When ready to serve, turn the broiler to high and set the rack so that a sheet pan with soup bowls can fit.

Ladle the soup into ovenproof soup crocks, leaving enough room for the bread and cheese. Place the crocks onto a baking sheet and place 2 pieces of bread, or enough to roughly cover the bowl in a single layer, on top of each bowl. Sprinkle the Gruyère atop the bread, dividing it evenly among the bowls.

Broil for 2 to 3 minutes or until the cheese is bubbly and browned. Garnish with thyme leaves and serve. Enjoy!

CLASSIC CHILI

MAKES: 6–8 SERVINGS • **PREP:** 15 MINUTES • **COOK:** 2 HOURS, 15 MINUTES

I've been making beef and bean chili in our home for years now, and every time I make it a little differently. Sometimes I'll add a little cinnamon, other times a little extra heat; sometimes I'll use ground turkey, or even cubed chuck for a Chili Colorado. So this recipe for classic chili with ground beef is based on hundreds of chili test runs, culminating in a perfect recipe that I know you will love.

Whenever we have chili, we always prep a few different toppings so everyone can take what they want. Our favorites include diced white onion, shredded cheddar, sliced jalapeño, and sour cream.

FOR THE GROUND SPICE MIXTURE

2 dried ancho chiles, stems and seeds removed

2 dried chipotle chiles, stems and seeds removed

2 tablespoons chili powder (if not using whole dried chiles, increase to 5 tablespoons)

2 tablespoons ground cumin

2 teaspoons ground cinnamon

¼ cup (30 g) crushed tortilla chips

FOR THE CHILI

¼ cup (60 ml) neutral oil, such as avocado oil, divided

1 large onion, diced

2 pounds (908 g) ground chuck

¼ cup water

1 (6-ounce) can tomato paste

2 tablespoons (26 g) granulated sugar

1 tablespoon garlic powder

2 teaspoons fine sea salt

3 (16-ounce) cans kidney beans, drained but not rinsed

2 cups (480 ml) low-sodium beef stock

1 (12-ounce) bottle Guinness

1½ ounces (42 g) 70% dark chocolate

Cayenne pepper, optional (see notes opposite)

FOR THE GROUND SPICE MIXTURE

Toast the chiles in a dry pan over medium heat for 30 seconds per side or until fragrant. Remove the chiles to a plate, then add the chili powder, cumin, and cinnamon to the pan and toast for 1 minute, stirring frequently.

Place the peppers, chili powder mixture, and tortilla chips into a food processor or coffee or spice grinder and blend until a fine powder is formed. Set aside.

FOR THE CHILI

Preheat the oven to 300°F and set the rack to the middle level, with enough room to accommodate a large Dutch oven and its lid.

Heat 2 tablespoons of the oil in a large Dutch oven over medium heat and sauté the onion until soft, 5 to 7 minutes.

Turn up the heat to medium-high, add the ground chuck, and sauté until browned while breaking it up with a wooden spoon or meat masher, about 7 minutes.

While the beef is cooking, bloom the spice mixture. Heat a small pan over medium heat and add the remaining 2 tablespoons of oil along with the prepared spice mixture. Cook for 1 to 2 minutes or until very fragrant, then add the water to the pan.

Once the beef is browned, add the bloomed spice mix to the beef and continue to cook for another minute, stirring to incorporate.

Add the tomato paste and cook for 3 minutes, stirring well to combine. Next, add the sugar, garlic powder, and salt and mix well.

Add the beans, beef stock, and Guinness and bring to a boil. Once boiling, give it all a stir, then turn the heat off and cover. Place the Dutch oven in the oven for 75 minutes.

After 75 minutes, remove the lid and return to the oven for another 30 to 45 minutes or until the chili has thickened. For a thicker chili, cook uncovered for another 30 minutes. Alternatively, place the pot on a burner and cook over medium heat until it thickens to your liking.

Remove the pot from the oven and add the chocolate, stirring to combine. Taste the chili and adjust the salt and spice levels to taste. An easy way to bring up the spice level quickly is with cayenne to taste. Serve in bowls with desired toppings.

The single most important thing you can do to improve your chili is to make it one day in advance and refrigerate overnight! The flavors will be so much better.

How much cayenne to use or whether to omit it completely will depend on the spice level of the dried chiles and commercial chili powder you use. For this reason, it's recommended to wait until the end before adding the cayenne.

Anaheim, pasilla, or guajillo peppers can be substituted for the ancho chiles.

Two dried ancho chiles equal approximately 2 tablespoons of chili powder and 2 dried chipotles equal approximately 1 tablespoon of chili powder. If you're only using ground chili powder, increase the amount from 2 to 5 tablespoons total.

Freshly grinding whole dried chiles will yield maximum flavor.

SALADS

Whether it's a crisp and refreshing end to a meal, a tasty appetizer or side to complement a main course, or a full-fledged meal itself, salad is a wonderful way to incorporate lightness and brightness into any meal.

In this chapter you'll find a variety of different salads, each with their own vinaigrette or dressing. Feel free to mix and match the vinaigrettes with the salads to suit your taste. If you want to use the creamy balsamic vinaigrette from our Harvest Salad (page 192) for your Sunday Dinner Salad (page 191), go for it. This is yet another opportunity for you to play around with flavors and textures and see what you like best.

THE SUNDAY DINNER SALAD

MAKES: 6–8 SERVINGS • PREP: 15 MINUTES

The Sunday Dinner Salad is a no-frills salad that serves as the perfect accompaniment to The Italian American Sunday Dinner (page 108).

While I was lucky enough to live with and learn from my Italian grandma, Tara lost hers when she was only seven years old. Her limited but fond memories of Grandma Jane include her hearty laugh and the amazing food she'd make for Sunday dinners, most notably her meatballs with sauce and her salad. Luckily, she taught her daughter-in-law (Tara's mom, Linda) to make these recipes and many others.

We've made a few tweaks here, opting for extra virgin olive oil and avocado oil over vegetable oil, which was used in abundance back in the seventies. Jane's dressing included Regina brand "garlic-flavored red wine vinegar"; we use plain red wine vinegar and add our own freshly grated garlic. Interestingly enough, Grandma Jane's salad is nearly identical to the salad I grew up eating, and the salad my mom still makes to this day.

FOR THE VINAIGRETTE

½ cup (120 ml) extra virgin olive oil

½ cup (120 ml) avocado oil, or other neutral oil

½ cup (120 ml) red wine vinegar

3 tablespoons (18 g) grated Parmigiano-Reggiano cheese

2 teaspoons Dijon mustard

2 teaspoons dried oregano

2 cloves garlic, grated

Salt and pepper, to taste

FOR THE SALAD

1 head iceberg lettuce, chopped and core removed

1 romaine lettuce heart, chopped

2 celery ribs, thinly sliced

1 small red onion, thinly sliced

1 large beefsteak tomato, cut into chunks

1 cucumber, sliced

4 radishes, thinly sliced

Salt and pepper, to taste

10 pepperoncini

FOR THE VINAIGRETTE

In a mason jar, add both the oils, the vinegar, cheese, mustard, oregano, and garlic. Place the lid on the jar and shake until the ingredients are combined and the dressing is emulsified. Taste-test and add salt and pepper as needed.

FOR THE SALAD

Place the iceberg and romaine lettuces in a large bowl or serving platter and top with the celery, onion, tomato, cucumber, and radishes.

Drizzle half the vinaigrette over the salad and toss to combine. Taste-test and again add salt and pepper as needed. Top with the pepperoncini and serve immediately with extra dressing on the side.

Feel free to add or subtract ingredients here. Some other common additions include shaved carrot, black olives, sliced green or red bell pepper, or Roasted Red Peppers (page 30). You can also use garlic powder to taste in place of the fresh garlic cloves.

Be sure to taste-test the salad after *it's dressed and add more salt and pepper if needed.*

HARVEST SALAD

MAKES: 4–6 SERVINGS • **PREP:** 15 MINUTES • **COOK:** 35 MINUTES

This hearty salad was inspired by some of our favorite fall flavors and ingredients.

With goat cheese, almonds, dried cranberries, roasted sweet potatoes, arugula, and homemade balsamic vinaigrette, plus farro for some bulk, this simple salad can easily pull duty as a full meal, but it is also excellent served alongside roasted chicken, steak, or broiled salmon.

FOR THE ROASTED VEGETABLES

2 large sweet potatoes, peeled and cut into 1-inch cubes

1 large red onion, sliced

¼ cup (60 ml) extra virgin olive oil

Salt and pepper, to taste

FOR THE VINAIGRETTE

½ cup (120 ml) balsamic vinegar

1 tablespoon (15 ml) honey, plus more to taste

1½ teaspoons Dijon mustard

1 large shallot, minced

1 teaspoon dried thyme

½ cup (120 ml) extra virgin olive oil

½ cup (120 ml) neutral oil, such as avocado oil

Salt and pepper, to taste

FOR THE SALAD

1¼ cups (250 g) uncooked pearled farro

2 cups (80 g) arugula

1 cup (140 g) sliced raw almonds

½ cup (70 g) dried cranberries

Salt and pepper, to taste

1 cup (140 g) crumbled goat cheese

FOR THE ROASTED VEGETABLES

Preheat the oven to 425°F and set the rack to the middle level. Line a baking sheet with parchment paper.

In a large bowl, toss the sweet potatoes and onion with the olive oil and season with salt and pepper to taste. Spread the vegetables out onto the parchment-lined baking sheet and roast, flipping the potatoes at the halfway point, until the sweet potatoes are fork-tender, 30 to 35 minutes. Let the vegetables cool for at least 5 minutes before adding to the salad.

FOR THE VINAIGRETTE

Combine the balsamic vinegar, honey, mustard, shallot, and thyme in a blender or food processor and pulse to combine.

Add both oils and blend until smooth and emulsified. Taste the vinaigrette and season with salt and pepper to taste, and if needed, more honey.

FOR THE SALAD

Bring a pot of salted water to boil and add the farro. Reduce the heat to a simmer and cook until tender, 15 to 25 minutes. Drain the cooked farro and rinse under cold water to cool it off.

Combine the farro, roasted sweet potatoes and onions, arugula, almonds, and cranberries in a large bowl and drizzle with one-third of the vinaigrette to start. Taste-test and, if needed, add more vinaigrette. Season with salt and pepper to taste. Add the goat cheese and serve immediately.

Feel free to add other ingredients here, such as butternut squash, brussels sprouts, carrots, parsnips, and pomegranate arils. Roasted beets would also be great.

If you are not a fan of goat cheese, you can use feta or even cubed mozzarella in its place.

Extra balsamic vinaigrette can be stored in the refrigerator for up to 5 days.

SICILIAN FENNEL AND ORANGE SALAD

MAKES: 4–6 SERVINGS • **PREP:** 20 MINUTES • **COOK:** 5 MINUTES

This Sicilian-style salad consists of the simplest ingredients, but yields a bright and flavorful dish that's refreshing, delicious, and beautiful to look at.

Fennel is a key ingredient and flavor in this dish, and it's important to note that the entire bulb is edible, as are the stalks and the fronds. The fronds make a gorgeous garnish at the end. Since fennel is purported to aid in digestion, we typically serve this salad at the end of a meal.

INGREDIENTS

1 small onion, thinly sliced

1 large fennel bulb, thinly sliced

5 medium oranges, peeled and segmented or sliced into ½-inch disks

1 lemon, juiced

¼ cup (60 ml) extra virgin olive oil

¼ cup (35 g) pignoli nuts

Fennel fronds, chopped, for garnish

1 teaspoon flaky sea salt

INSTRUCTIONS

In a medium bowl, toss the onion and fennel together and place on a serving dish. Layer the orange slices on top of the fennel and onion slices.

In a small bowl, whisk together the lemon juice and olive oil, then drizzle on top of the fennel, onion, and orange mixture.

Toast the pignoli nuts in a small, dry pan over low heat until fragrant and golden, 3 to 5 minutes, paying close attention to prevent them from burning.

Remove the nuts from the pan, and once cool, sprinkle on top of the orange-fennel salad.

Top the salad with the chopped fennel fronds and flaky sea salt and serve.

This salad travels well and can be made a few hours ahead of time. If you don't plan to serve it immediately, hold off on adding the flaky sea salt until you're ready to serve. It has a tendency to dissolve into the oranges and you'll have better results if you wait.

Any variety of orange will work here. Feel free to use any combination of blood orange, navel, or cara cara, or even grapefruit!

Variations of this salad will often include oil-cured olives, fresh mint, or basil, so feel free to experiment.

SIP & FEAST TIPS

PANZANELLA SALAD

MAKES: 6–8 SERVINGS • **PREP:** 20 MINUTES • **COOK:** 15 MINUTES • **REST:** 45 MINUTES

The first time I ever had panzanella salad, I wondered where this amazing dish had been all my life! It wasn't until I was in my early twenties that I first had it. Tara's stepmother, Angelina, had made it for us and I was amazed at just how delicious and flavorful day-old bread could be. Since then I've been making my own version, but I'd be remiss to say it wasn't inspired by Angie's!

Panzanella is best in the summer alongside grilled meat, chicken, or fish, but it can certainly be enjoyed all year round.

FOR THE VINAIGRETTE

¾ cup (180 ml) extra virgin olive oil, plus more as needed

¼ cup (60 ml) red wine vinegar

2 cloves garlic, minced

1 teaspoon Dijon mustard

1 teaspoon dried oregano

Salt and pepper, to taste

FOR THE SALAD

1 pound (454 g) crusty Italian or rustic bread, cut into 1-inch cubes

2 pounds (908 g) ripe beefsteak or large heirloom tomatoes, chopped into 1½-inch pieces

Salt, to taste

1 medium red onion, thinly sliced

½ cup packed basil leaves

FOR THE VINAIGRETTE

Whisk all the vinaigrette ingredients together and season with salt and pepper to taste. Alternatively, pulse in a blender or food processor until smooth.

FOR THE SALAD

If you are using day-old bread that is very firm, you can skip the toasting process. For fresh bread, preheat the oven to 325°F and lay the bread cubes out on a baking sheet. Toast the bread until it's hard on the outside, 12 to 15 minutes.

Toss the tomatoes with the vinaigrette in a large bowl and season liberally with salt. Let them sit for 15 minutes before mixing in the other ingredients.

Add the bread and onions to the bowl and mix well. If needed, add a few more tablespoons of extra virgin olive oil. Let the salad sit for at least 30 minutes, tossing every so often, before eating. Right before serving mix in the basil leaves and toss one more time.

Allowing the tomatoes to initially absorb the vinaigrette and macerate is important so that the juice from the tomatoes and vinaigrette will more readily absorb into the bread.

Don't rush. Let the panzanella sit for a good 20 to 30 minutes before eating.

Cucumber, mozzarella balls, and plenty of other ingredients can be added to this salad.

SPINACH SALAD WITH HOT BACON DRESSING

MAKES: 6–8 SERVINGS • **PREP:** 10 MINUTES • **COOK:** 15 MINUTES

Spinach salad with hot bacon dressing is a dish I learned from my mom. She'd often make it for holidays and it always got rave reviews.

The vinaigrette includes bacon fat, shallots, and Dijon mustard and is just hot enough to slightly wilt the baby spinach and the raw mushrooms and sliced red onions, adding wonderful texture and flavor.

Since it's such a crowd-pleaser, we often make it for gatherings, but it's so great we also make it during the week with some soup and crusty bread.

INGREDIENTS

½ pound (226 g) bacon, cut into ½-inch pieces

¾ pound (340 g) baby spinach

¾ pound (340 g) white or cremini mushrooms, sliced

1 small red onion, sliced

½ cup (120 ml) extra virgin olive oil

1 large shallot, minced

5 tablespoons (75 ml) red wine vinegar

1½ tablespoons (22 ml) honey

2 teaspoons Dijon mustard

1 tablespoon (6 g) grated pecorino Romano cheese

Salt and pepper, to taste

INSTRUCTIONS

In a large nonstick pan over medium heat, cook the bacon until crisp, about 10 minutes, then remove with a slotted spoon to a paper towel–lined plate to drain. Pour off all but 5 tablespoons (75 ml) of the bacon fat for the dressing.

Place the spinach, mushrooms, and onion in a large salad bowl.

In the same pan that was used for the bacon, heat the reserved bacon fat and the olive oil over medium-low heat and cook the shallots until soft, 3 to 4 minutes.

Add the vinegar, honey, mustard, and cheese to the pan and whisk together. Add salt and pepper to taste. Turn the heat down to low but keep the dressing warm.

Sprinkle half of the bacon and pour half of the dressing onto the salad and toss well. Add a bit more dressing if needed, but don't overdress it. Serve the remaining dressing on the side and top each plate with the remaining bacon.

If making ahead, do not dress the salad until you're ready to serve. Be sure to heat the dressing again right before serving.

A hearty green like kale would do well in place of the spinach, as it can hold up nicely to the heat of the dressing. It's not recommended to use more delicate greens, as they may wilt too much.

CLASSIC CHICKEN CAESAR SALAD

MAKES: 4–6 SERVINGS • **PREP:** 15 MINUTES • **COOK:** 20 MINUTES

I've always loved Caesar salad and we'd regularly order it in Italian family-style restaurants, but I had never made it at home since it always seemed too complicated for just a salad. Until one day I decided to try making it and realized how incredibly easy it is, and that it actually tastes way better when made at home!

Our version of this tried-and-true classic includes pan-seared chicken and homemade garlic croutons, both of which make this salad substantial enough to be a full meal.

FOR THE CROUTONS

- 3 cups (150 g) cubed bread, 1-inch cubes
- 3 tablespoons (45 ml) extra virgin olive oil
- 2 tablespoons (13 g) grated Parmigiano-Reggiano cheese
- ½ teaspoon garlic powder
- ½ teaspoon kosher salt
- ¼ teaspoon ground black pepper

FOR THE CHICKEN

- 1½ pounds (680 g) thin-sliced chicken cutlets
- 1 teaspoon kosher salt
- ½ teaspoon ground black pepper
- 2 tablespoons (30 ml) extra virgin olive oil

FOR THE DRESSING

- 6 anchovies, mashed into a paste
- 2 large pasteurized egg yolks (see notes below)
- 2 tablespoons (30 ml) fresh lemon juice
- 1 teaspoon Worcestershire sauce
- 1 clove garlic, grated
- ½ cup (120 ml) extra virgin olive oil
- Salt and pepper, to taste

FOR THE SALAD

- 3 heads romaine lettuce, outer leaves removed, torn into 3-inch-long pieces
- 3 tablespoons (18 g) shredded Parmigiano-Reggiano cheese
- Shaved Parmigiano-Reggiano cheese, for finishing

FOR THE CROUTONS

Preheat the oven to 350°F. Line a baking sheet with parchment paper. Toss all the crouton ingredients together in a large bowl. Spread the croutons onto the parchment-lined baking sheet and bake for 10 minutes or until lightly toasted.

FOR THE CHICKEN

Heat a large stainless steel pan over medium heat. Pat the chicken dry with paper towels and season with the salt and pepper. Add the olive oil to the pan and sear the chicken until cooked through, 3 to 4 minutes per side. Place the cooked chicken onto a cutting board, cover with tented foil, and set aside. After 5 minutes of resting, slice the chicken into thin strips.

FOR THE DRESSING

Combine the anchovies, egg yolks, lemon juice, Worcestershire, and garlic in a food processor. Turn the processor on and slowly drizzle the olive oil through the top and blend until emulsified. Taste-test and season the dressing with salt and pepper to taste. *Note:* The dressing can also be hand whisked or can be prepared in a wide-mouthed mason jar using an immersion blender.

FOR THE SALAD

Place the lettuce into a large bowl and spoon 3 to 4 tablespoons of the dressing over to start, along with most of the croutons and all of the shredded cheese. Toss well to coat. If extra dressing is needed, add more to your liking and toss again.

Place the tossed salad onto a large platter and lay the chicken strips on top. Sprinkle the remaining croutons over the salad and use a vegetable peeler to shave a bit of extra cheese over the top. Spoon more of the dressing onto the chicken if desired, or serve at the table.

For safety reasons, we recommend using pasteurized egg yolks. Or you can add a bit of lemon juice to unpasteurized yolks and gently heat them to 135°F, which will kill any bacteria without cooking the eggs.

If you prefer to omit the anchovies, you can do so, but know that you may need to increase the salt used in the dressing, as anchovies are quite salty. On the other hand, if you love anchovies, feel free to add some whole anchovies to the top of your salad for extra flavor.

We use olive oil for our dressing, but the original Caesar was made using vegetable oil. Feel free to use whichever oil you prefer. If, after blending, the dressing is too thick, add a teaspoon or two of water to loosen it. Conversely, if the dressing is too thin, add a touch more oil.

ITALIAN POTATO AND GREEN BEAN SALAD

MAKES: 6–8 SERVINGS • **PREP:** 15 MINUTES • **COOK:** 15 MINUTES • **REST:** 10 MINUTES

There's no salad more symbolic of summer than Italian potato and green bean salad. The warm potatoes are tossed with razor-thin sliced red onion in a simple vinaigrette and finished with cherry tomatoes, green beans, and fresh herbs. It's loaded with flavor and incredibly rustic.

If you know several different Italian American families, you may notice that every one of them has their own variation of this salad, but the base will always include potatoes, green beans, and vinaigrette.

We serve this for summer dinners and gatherings, and it's particularly good alongside grilled meat and burgers.

FOR THE VINAIGRETTE

- ½ cup (120 ml) extra virgin olive oil
- ½ cup (120 ml) red wine vinegar
- 1 tablespoon (15 ml) honey
- 1½ teaspoons Dijon mustard
- ¼ cup minced flat-leaf Italian parsley
- Salt and pepper, to taste

FOR THE SALAD

- 1 cup (150 g) thinly sliced red onion
- 3 pounds (1.4 kg) red potatoes, cut into 1½-inch cubes
- ¾ pound (340 g) green beans, stems removed, cut into 3-inch pieces
- ¾ pound (340 g) cherry tomatoes, halved
- ¼ cup packed basil leaves, hand torn

FOR THE VINAIGRETTE

In a large bowl, whisk together all the vinaigrette ingredients.

FOR THE SALAD

Add the onions to the bowl of vinaigrette, mix, and set aside.

Add the potatoes to a pot of salted water and bring to a boil. Cook until the potatoes are a few minutes from fork-tender, 10 to 12 minutes, and then add the green beans. Continue to cook until the green beans are bright green and the potatoes are almost fork-tender, 3 to 5 more minutes.

Remove the green beans with a slotted spoon and set them aside. Drain the potatoes in a colander.

Place the warm potatoes into the vinaigrette with the onions and toss to coat. Next, add the green beans and toss them together. Taste-test and make any final adjustments to the salt and pepper if required. Let the potatoes and green beans sit in the vinaigrette for at least 10 minutes to better absorb the flavors.

Right before serving, add the cherry tomatoes and basil on top and gently mix one more time.

You can use any waxy potato, such as Yukon Gold or red potatoes. Depending on the size, you may only need to cut them in half, or if they're larger you'll need to cut into quarters or eighths until they're approximately 1½-inch cubes. It's important not to overcook the potatoes so they remain intact.

Opt for the freshest beans you can find. Often they'll be in a large bin in the grocery store and you can hand select the best ones, or you can buy them already bagged. It's not recommend to use frozen or canned green beans for this salad.

It's best to have the vinaigrette already made and waiting, along with the red onions, so the potatoes can be tossed with the vinaigrette while they're hot. This helps them to readily absorb the vinaigrette.

This salad can be eaten right away, but letting it sit for 2 hours or even overnight will help the potatoes better absorb the flavors. If refrigerating overnight, hold back on adding the tomatoes until the day it is served so that they don't become mushy.

SIP & FEAST TIPS

COLD BROCCOLI SALAD

MAKES: 4 SERVINGS • **PREP:** 5 MINUTES • **COOK:** 10 MINUTES • **REST:** 1 HOUR

This Italian broccoli salad is a dish we've been eating for years! My grandma would make this all the time when I was a kid, and now I make it for my family.

The lemon zest marries perfectly with the broccoli, and the lemon-garlic vinaigrette is simple but incredibly tasty. Since this salad is best served cold, I'll often make a large batch of it and we'll enjoy it all week long.

INGREDIENTS

1 head broccoli, bottom 2 inches of stem discarded and the rest broken into small florets

½ cup (120 ml) extra virgin olive oil

¼ cup (60 ml) fresh lemon juice, plus more to taste

1 teaspoon Dijon mustard

5 cloves garlic, minced

¼ teaspoon crushed hot red pepper flakes, plus more to taste

1 tablespoon (6 g) lemon zest

Salt, to taste

INSTRUCTIONS

Bring a large pot of water to boil. Once boiling, add the broccoli and cook until almost tender, 5 to 6 minutes, then drain but do *not* rinse to cool.

Meanwhile, in a large bowl, whisk the olive oil, lemon juice, mustard, garlic, and red pepper flakes together until emulsified.

Add the warm broccoli to the bowl with the dressing and toss with the lemon zest until well combined. Taste-test and season well with salt. If needed, add more lemon juice or hot pepper flakes.

Let the broccoli salad sit in the fridge for 1 hour to adequately absorb the dressing. If possible, refrigerate overnight, which will make the flavors stronger.

Don't rinse the broccoli after it's cooked. Adding the dressing and lemon zest to the broccoli while it's warm helps intensify the flavor.

Since there are so few ingredients in this salad, it's recommended that you use fresh broccoli, fresh lemon juice, and fresh garlic along with your best extra virgin olive oil.

Wait a minimum of 1 hour before eating to let the flavors absorb into the broccoli.

SIP & FEAST TIPS

SWEETS

When I think back on childhood holidays and gatherings, the dessert table always stands out. Everyone would bring something—there would be a variety of cookies and pastries from the Italian bakery, homemade cakes and pies, donuts, ice cream, and more. For a kid, it was a dream come true.

It's with a childlike spirit that Tara and I curated this chapter. We wanted a little something for every occasion, from holidays and gatherings to birthdays and quiet nights at home when you just want to treat yourself to something sweet. After all, a feast isn't a feast unless it's capped off with an outstanding dessert, and perhaps an espresso (or double espresso!).

Take care not to oversoak the ladyfingers; they only need 1 second per side. You'll most likely have leftover espresso–coffee liqueur mixture.

The alcohol can easily be omitted from both the coffee mixture and the zabaglione.

Use an instant-read thermometer for accurate temperature reading on the zabaglione.

You can sprinkle the cocoa on top before placing the tiramisu in the refrigerator, but the top layer of the filling may absorb some of it, changing the color slightly. We prefer to use a fresh dusting of cocoa right before slicing and serving the tiramisu.

SIP & FEAST TIPS

TIRAMISU

MAKES: 12 SERVINGS • **PREP:** 20 MINUTES • **COOK:** 10 MINUTES • **CHILL:** 6 HOURS

With its layers of espresso-dipped ladyfingers, whipped mascarpone-zabaglione cream, and cocoa powder, this classic Italian dessert is one you'll want to make again and again, especially if you are a coffee lover.

If you've made other tiramisu recipes, you may notice that some call for uncooked eggs, and others for rum or other liquor. When we created our version of the recipe, we combined a variety of different flavors and techniques to yield the best-tasting tiramisu we've ever had.

Tiramisu is the perfect dessert for holidays and gatherings, especially alongside an Espresso Martini (page 247)!

FOR THE ESPRESSO MIXTURE

- ¾ cup (180 ml) espresso, as needed
- ⅓ cup (80 ml) coffee liqueur, as needed

FOR THE MASCARPONE FILLING

- 1 pound (454 g) mascarpone cheese, at room temperature
- 6 large egg yolks, at room temperature
- ¼ cup (60 ml) Marsala wine
- ¾ cup (150 g) granulated sugar
- 2 cups (480 ml) heavy cream
- 2 teaspoons vanilla extract

FOR ASSEMBLY

- 40 savoiardi (ladyfingers)
- ¼ cup (22 g) unsweetened cocoa powder

FOR THE ESPRESSO MIXTURE

In a shallow bowl, combine the espresso and coffee liqueur and set aside.

FOR THE MASCARPONE FILLING

In a large bowl, whisk the mascarpone until light, about 2 minutes, and set aside.

Combine the egg yolks, Marsala, and sugar in a double boiler or glass bowl over a pot of simmering (not boiling) water and whisk to create a zabaglione. Be careful not to let the bottom of the bowl touch the water. Whisk the yolks and sugar over the heat until the combination has thickened and coats the back of a spoon, about 10 minutes. The temperature of the yolks should reach approximately 160°F.

Allow the zabaglione to cool for a few minutes, then add to the mascarpone and fold until just combined.

In a large mixing bowl or the bowl of a stand mixer fitted with the whisk attachment, beat the heavy cream and vanilla extract on low, then gradually move to high speed and beat until the cream has medium-stiff peaks, taking care not to overmix.

Fold half of the whipped cream into the mascarpone-zabaglione mixture, then add the remaining whipped cream and gently fold until just incorporated.

FOR ASSEMBLY

Dip both sides of the ladyfingers into the espresso mixture, taking care not to oversoak, and place them side by side in a 9-x-13-inch baking dish until you've formed one even layer. If needed, cut a few to fit so there are no gaps.

Spoon half of the mascarpone mixture onto the ladyfingers and use a spatula to smooth it out. Sprinkle with a dusting of cocoa powder.

Continue to the next layer, dipping and arranging the ladyfingers side by side. Once finished, spoon and smooth the remaining mascarpone mixture on top, cover, and set in the refrigerator for at least 6 hours, but preferably overnight.

Right before serving, dust the tiramisu with the remaining cocoa powder. Using a sharp knife, slice into squares and serve.

PANNA COTTA WITH FRESH BERRIES

MAKES: 6–8 SERVINGS • **PREP:** 5 MINUTES • **COOK:** 10 MINUTES • **CHILL:** 4 HOURS

Tara has been making panna cotta for years, usually when we have guests, and it's always such a hit. Depending on who we're having, she will often change the flavors and toppings. At times she'll add rosewater and cardamom and top with chopped pistachios, or she'll use millefiori extract or fiori di Sicilia and top with orange zest and toasted pignoli nuts.

But this classic version is the one she makes most often, and it's my favorite version. The creamy texture and vanilla flavor are traditional and pair perfectly with the fresh berries. If you can't find fresh berries, feel free to use frozen berries that have been thawed.

INGREDIENTS

¼ cup (60 ml) whole milk

1 tablespoon (15 g) unflavored powdered gelatin

3 cups (720 ml) heavy cream

⅓ cup (66 g) granulated sugar

1 pinch fine sea salt

1 vanilla bean, seeds scraped

2 cups (300 g) assorted berries

INSTRUCTIONS

Place the milk in a medium bowl, sprinkle the gelatin over the top, and allow it to sit for 5 to 10 minutes.

Meanwhile, combine the cream, sugar, salt, and vanilla seeds in a medium pot over medium heat and stir just until the sugar dissolves, 5 to 7 minutes.

Reduce the heat to low, add the gelatin-milk mixture, and whisk until smooth and the gelatin is fully dissolved. Take care not to allow the mixture to boil.

Using a ladle, pour an even amount of the mixture into each of 6 to 8 individual glasses. Allow to cool slightly before placing in the refrigerator to set for at least 4 hours, but preferably overnight.

Top with fresh berries right before serving and enjoy.

You can use 2 teaspoons of vanilla extract in place of the vanilla bean seeds.

The blueberry sauce we use on our Italian Cheesecake (page 213) would be an excellent topping here in place of, or in addition to, the fresh berries.

Draining the ricotta overnight through a cheesecloth or fine-mesh sieve is required to ensure the cheesecake isn't runny and bakes properly.

When beating egg whites, it's imperative not to allow any of the yolk (the fat) or any other grease to come in contact with the whites, otherwise they'll never stand up no matter how long you beat them.

Using a water bath, also known as a bain-marie, helps to gently cook the cheesecake and to prevent sudden temperature changes that can lead to cracking or deflating. It's helpful to place the roasting pan with the cheesecake on the rack in the oven before adding the water, then pull the rack out enough to allow you to fill the roasting pan from a kettle of hot water. That way you're not transporting the entire pan filled with hot water to the oven. We strongly recommend following our process to avoid cracks, beginning with the bain-marie and then reducing the temperature after 10 minutes of cooking and allowing the cake to cool in the oven for 30 minutes with the door cracked. Also, avoid making sudden hard movements near and around the oven while the cheesecake is there.

Since this cheesecake has no crust, it's harder to remove from the bottom plate. Use a paper insert (or cut one from parchment paper) to make removing the cheesecake easier, or you can leave the cheesecake on the springform's bottom for serving.

This recipe was written for a conventional oven. For convection ovens, reduce the temperature by 25°F and begin checking for doneness at the 34-minute mark.

ITALIAN CHEESECAKE

MAKES: 8 SERVINGS • **PREP:** 20 MINUTES • **COOK:** 55 MINUTES • **COOL AND CHILL:** 6½ HOURS

Italian cheesecake has always been a favorite in our home. Thanks to the ricotta, its texture is lighter than that of a New York–style cheesecake, and the orange zest takes the flavor over the top. This recipe includes instructions for a lemon-blueberry sauce that perfectly complements the flavor of the cheesecake, but you can definitely serve it plain if preferred.

This dessert is perfect for holidays, gatherings, birthdays, or any time you want a little bit of decadence!

FOR THE CHEESECAKE

- Butter, for greasing the pan
- 2 pounds (908 g) whole-milk ricotta cheese, drained overnight (see notes opposite)
- 1 cup (200 g) granulated sugar, divided
- 5 large egg yolks, at room temperature
- ¼ cup (35 g) all-purpose flour, sifted, plus more for dusting
- 2 large navel oranges, zested
- 1 teaspoon vanilla extract
- 5 large egg whites, at room temperature

FOR THE BLUEBERRY SAUCE

- 10 ounces (290 g) frozen blueberries
- ½ cup (120 ml) water
- ½ cup (100 g) granulated sugar
- 1 teaspoon vanilla extract
- 1½ tablespoons (11 g) cornstarch, dissolved in 1½ tablespoons (22 ml) water
- 1 large lemon, zested

FOR THE CHEESECAKE

Preheat your oven to 400°F and use butter to grease the bottom and sides of a 10-inch springform pan. If desired, place a paper insert in the bottom of the pan, or use a piece of parchment paper cut to fit the bottom (see notes opposite).

Wrap the outside edges of the springform pan with two layers of foil and place in a roasting pan.

In a large bowl or the bowl of a stand mixer fitted with the whisk attachment, beat the ricotta on medium-low speed until smooth, gradually adding ⅔ cup of the sugar and the egg yolks one at a time, beating after each addition. Add the flour, orange zest, and vanilla and mix until combined.

In a separate large bowl, beat the egg whites for 30 seconds, then gradually add the remaining ⅓ cup of sugar while beating on medium speed. Once all the sugar is added, beat on high speed until medium-soft peaks are formed.

Using a spatula, fold the egg whites into the ricotta mixture, taking care not to overmix, then add the mixture to the prepared springform pan. Add enough hot water to the roasting pan to cover the bottom half of the springform pan for your water bath.

Bake for 10 minutes at 400°F, then reduce the heat to 325°F and bake for 45 minutes until golden on top and slightly jiggly in the center.

Turn off the heat and allow the cheesecake to cool in the oven for 30 minutes with the door cracked. Remove from the oven and run a thin-bladed knife around the edge of the cake to keep it from sticking to the sides. Allow the cake to come to room temperature, then cover and move to the refrigerator for a minimum of 6 hours. Once chilled, remove the cake from the springform pan. Slice and serve with the blueberry sauce on the side.

FOR THE BLUEBERRY SAUCE

Place the blueberries, water, sugar, and vanilla in a small saucepan and cook over medium heat until the mixture comes to a slow boil.

Stir in the cornstarch mixture and bring to a rolling boil, then turn the heat down and simmer for 1 to 2 minutes or until the mixture reaches your desired consistency.

Remove from the heat and gently stir in the lemon zest, taking care not to crush the blueberries.

Drizzle over the cooled cheesecake.

CHOCOLATE CHIP RICOTTA CAKE

MAKES: 8 SERVINGS • **PREP:** 15 MINUTES • **COOK:** 50 MINUTES • **COOL:** 30 MINUTES

This truly is one of the easiest cakes you can make. With no mixer required, this simple dessert comes together in no time! Its creamy texture and combination of ricotta, chocolate chips, and just a hint of cinnamon is reminiscent of cannoli cream.

It's simple enough to throw together for an impromptu gathering, but it is decadent enough to serve for holidays and special occasions. I've even been known to eat a slice for breakfast.

INGREDIENTS

Butter or cooking spray, for greasing the pan

1 cup (130 g) all-purpose flour

1 teaspoon baking powder

½ teaspoon fine sea salt

1 teaspoon ground cinnamon

3 large eggs, at room temperature

¾ cup (150 g) granulated sugar

8 tablespoons (113 g) butter, melted and cooled

20 ounces (566 g) whole-milk ricotta cheese (see notes below)

1 tablespoon (15 ml) white crème de cacao

2 teaspoons vanilla extract

¾ cup (127 g) mini chocolate chips, divided

Confectioners' sugar, for dusting

INSTRUCTIONS

Preheat the oven to 350°F and prepare a 9-inch springform pan by greasing the sides and lining the bottom with parchment paper.

In a medium bowl, combine the flour, baking powder, salt, and cinnamon.

In a large bowl, whisk together the eggs and sugar until light and frothy.

Add the melted butter to the egg mixture and whisk until incorporated, then add the ricotta, crème de cacao, and vanilla and whisk until combined.

Slowly add the dry ingredients and mix just until combined, then fold in ½ cup of the mini chocolate chips.

Place the prepared springform pan on a baking sheet, pour the batter into the pan, and smooth the top with a spatula. Sprinkle the remaining mini chocolate chips on top.

Bake for 45 to 50 minutes until the cake is golden brown and a toothpick inserted in the center comes out clean.

Allow the cake to cool on a wire rack for at least 30 minutes before removing from the springform pan. Dust with confectioners' sugar before serving.

If you're using a very wet ricotta, like Polly-O brand, you should drain the ricotta through a cheesecloth to remove excess liquid. If you're using a drier ricotta, such as Galbani, draining may not be necessary.

You can omit the crème de cacao and replace it with an additional teaspoon of vanilla extract.

This recipe was written for a conventional oven. For convection ovens, reduce the temperature by 25°F and begin checking for doneness after 34 minutes.

This cake can be stored in the refrigerator for 3 to 5 days.

SIP & FEAST TIPS

GRAPEFRUIT OLIVE OIL CAKE

MAKES: 10 SERVINGS • **PREP:** 10 MINUTES • **COOK:** 55 MINUTES

Moist, delicious, and loaded with citrus vanilla flavor, this grapefruit olive oil cake is one for the books. It is so easy to make, and we have it at the top of our list when it comes to desserts to put out for company.

Opt for the grapefruit glaze, or serve it without; just be sure to enjoy it with a cup of coffee or espresso—it's a match made in heaven!

FOR THE CAKE

Olive oil or cooking spray, for greasing the pan

2 cups (260 g) all-purpose flour

1½ cups (300 g) granulated sugar

1 teaspoon kosher salt

½ teaspoon baking powder

½ teaspoon baking soda

1⅓ cups (320 ml) extra virgin olive oil

1¼ cups (300 ml) whole milk

3 large eggs

¼ cup (60 ml) fresh grapefruit juice

¼ cup (60 ml) Gran Gala orange liqueur

1 teaspoon vanilla extract

3 tablespoons (18 g) grapefruit zest

FOR THE GLAZE

1 cup (115 g) confectioners' sugar

2 tablespoons (30 ml) freshly squeezed grapefruit juice

¼ teaspoon vanilla extract

1 pinch sea salt

FOR THE CAKE

Preheat the oven to 350°F and set the rack to the middle level. Grease a 9-x-2-inch round cake pan and line the bottom with parchment paper.

In a medium bowl, combine the flour, sugar, salt, baking powder, and baking soda and stir until combined. Set aside.

In a large bowl, combine the olive oil, milk, eggs, grapefruit juice, Gran Gala, vanilla, and grapefruit zest and whisk until combined.

Add the dry ingredients to the wet ingredients and stir until just combined. The batter should be on the thinner side and easy to pour.

Pour the batter into the prepared cake pan and give the cake pan a tap to allow any air to rise to the top.

Place the cake pan in the oven and bake for 55 minutes or until a toothpick inserted in the center comes out clean.

Allow the cake to cool before adding the glaze or serving. If you're not using the glaze, serve plain or top with confectioners' sugar.

FOR THE GLAZE

Once the cake has cooled, in a mixing bowl combine the confectioners' sugar, grapefruit juice, vanilla extract, and salt and whisk until well combined.

Pour the glaze on top of the cake and allow the glaze to harden at room temperature for about 1 hour, or place in the refrigerator to speed up the process.

Because ovens can vary, begin checking the cake for doneness at the 50-minute mark.

This recipe was written for a conventional oven. For convection ovens, reduce the temperature by 25°F and begin checking for doneness after 37 minutes.

FLOURLESS CHOCOLATE CAKE

MAKES: 8 SERVINGS • **PREP:** 20 MINUTES • **COOK:** 30 MINUTES

Fudgy, decadent, and made with just a few ingredients, flourless chocolate cake is the dessert you'll make again and again. Because it's made with almond meal, aka almond flour, it's naturally gluten-free, and the incredibly rich texture and chocolate flavor are almost brownie-like, making this a dessert that is loved by nearly everyone.

Flourless chocolate cake is also known as torta Caprese, as it originated on the island of Capri. The recipe is really quite simple: equal parts by weight of almond flour, butter, sugar, and chocolate, 4 eggs, and some confectioners' sugar for dusting.

It's great for gatherings but also perfect for quiet evenings when your chocolate craving is strong!

INGREDIENTS

Butter or cooking spray, for greasing the pan

6.7 ounces (190 g) bittersweet chocolate, 50 to 80% cacao

13½ tablespoons (190 g) butter, cubed and softened to room temperature

2 cups (190 g) almond flour

1 cup (190 g) granulated sugar, divided

4 large eggs, separated, at room temperature

Confectioners' sugar, for dusting

INSTRUCTIONS

Preheat the oven to 350°F. Grease a 9-inch springform pan with butter or cooking spray and line the bottom with parchment paper.

In a double boiler or bowl set over a pan of simmering water, melt the chocolate. Once melted, remove from the heat, add the butter, and continue to stir while the butter melts.

Add the almond flour and ¾ cup of the sugar and continue to stir until combined.

Once the mixture has cooled, add the egg yolks and stir until combined.

In a separate clean bowl, or in the bowl of a stand mixer fitted with the whisk attachment, beat the egg whites for 30 seconds, then add the remaining ¼ cup sugar and beat on high until the whites reach medium peaks.

Using a rubber spatula, gently fold the whipped egg whites into the chocolate batter one-third at a time.

Pour the batter into the prepared cake pan and level with a spoon or offset spatula. Bake for 30 minutes or until a toothpick inserted into the center comes out with just a few moist crumbs. It does not need to be completely dry.

Allow the cake to cool in the pan on a wire rack before removing from the springform pan and dusting lightly with confectioners' sugar. Enjoy!

Using a kitchen scale allows for consistent results every time. You may measure a cup of sugar differently on one day than you would on another, whereas a scale measures exactly the same way each time. Since this cake calls for equal weight of everything (except the eggs), a scale is the way to go.

Use a springform pan to remove the cake more easily. Be sure to grease the sides and bottom of the pan, and line the bottom with parchment paper for even easier removal. Also, after baking, sliding a thin knife around the edges will help prevent any sticking.

This cake is better on the moister side, so be sure not to overcook. When checking for doneness, the toothpick should not be 100% dry.

This recipe was written for a conventional oven. For convection ovens, reduce the temperature by 25°F and begin checking for doneness after 22 minutes.

PIZZELLE

MAKES: 30 PIZZELLE • **PREP:** 10 MINUTES • **COOK:** 20 MINUTES

Italian pizzelle are a holiday favorite in our home, and every time I make them I wonder why I don't make them more often. These cookies are wonderful for Christmas or Easter, but they're easy enough to make all year long.

While they're great on their own with some confectioners' sugar, we will often use them as a cheat code for cannoli shells! To do this, wrap the pizzelle around a cannoli form or dowel when they come out of the iron and are still pliable. Once cool, fill the shells with cannoli cream and your favorite toppings!

INGREDIENTS

- 3½ cups (455 g) all-purpose flour
- 4 teaspoons (16 g) baking powder
- ½ teaspoon kosher salt
- 6 large eggs, at room temperature
- 1½ cups (300 g) granulated sugar
- 4 teaspoons (20 ml) anise extract
- 2 teaspoons vanilla extract
- 16 tablespoons (226 g) butter, melted and cooled to room temperature
- Cooking spray for the pizzelle iron
- ¼ cup (28 g) confectioners' sugar, for dusting, optional

INSTRUCTIONS

Preheat the pizzelle iron (see notes below). In a medium bowl, combine the flour, baking powder, and salt.

In a large bowl, whisk the eggs, granulated sugar, anise, and vanilla until smooth, then add the butter and whisk until combined.

Fold the flour mixture into the egg mixture just until blended, taking care not to overmix.

Spray the pizzelle iron with the cooking spray. Use a cookie scoop to place approximately 2 tablespoons of batter into each mold and close the lid.

Follow the manufacturer's instructions for cooking (we use a Palmer; it is 35 to 45 seconds or until steaming stops). Use a fork to remove and transfer the pizzelle to a wire rack to cool, and repeat the process with the remaining batter.

Once cooled, dust the pizzelle with the confectioners' sugar, if desired.

Traditional pizzelle are flavored with anise, which tastes a lot like licorice or sambuca. If you're not a fan of anise, you can skip that flavor and just increase the amount of vanilla, or experiment with other extracts, like almond, orange, or lemon.

Pizzelle require a pizzelle iron to achieve the waffle and star designs. We use a Palmer classic iron with aluminum plates, but since not all irons are the same, it's important for you to follow the manufacturer's instructions for preheating and cooking. Be sure to give the pizzelle iron ample time to warm up before using, and cool it down completely before storing again.

You may need one or two test runs with the pizzelle iron and batter before you make the perfect pizzelle. The most common problem is not loading enough batter, yielding an incomplete disk. After two attempts or so you'll get the hang of it. We've found that placing the batter toward the back third of the iron works best to evenly distribute the batter once the iron is closed and clamped. The batter will seep out from the sides of the iron, and that's normal! It means that you've placed enough batter on the iron.

Pizzelle can be stored at room temperature in an airtight container for up to 1 week.

SIP & FEAST TIPS

REGINA COOKIES

MAKES: 36 COOKIES • **PREP:** 20 MINUTES • **COOK:** 30 MINUTES • **REST:** 40 MINUTES

Regina cookies, also known as *reginelle*, are classic Italian cookies that can be found in nearly every Italian bakery in the New York metropolitan area. They also happen to be Tara's dad's favorite cookie of all time, which makes perfect sense. For as long as I've known Jerry, he's always appreciated the simple things in life, and every time I eat one of these cookies, I'm reminded that those simple things, more often than not, are the best things.

There's nothing flashy about regina cookies—no bright colors or sprinkles—but that's what makes them stand out. They're the perfect companion to a cup of coffee or espresso, and they are a welcome addition to any holiday cookie platter.

INGREDIENTS

2 cups (260 g) all-purpose flour

½ cup (100 g) granulated sugar

1 teaspoon baking powder

¼ teaspoon fine sea salt

8 tablespoons (113 g) butter, cubed and at room temperature

1 large egg, beaten and at room temperature

2 teaspoons lemon zest

¼ cup (60 ml) whole milk, plus more for the dough if needed

1 cup (142 g) raw sesame seeds

INSTRUCTIONS

In a large bowl, combine the flour, sugar, baking powder, and salt and mix until combined.

Using a pastry cutter or your hands, mix in the butter until the mixture resembles coarse crumbs.

Add the egg and lemon zest and mix until a dough forms. It will be crumbly. Using your hands, shape the dough into a ball. If it's too dry, add a tablespoon of milk. Once the dough ball is formed, cover it with plastic wrap and refrigerate it for at least 30 minutes.

Remove the dough and allow it to rest for 10 minutes at room temperature. Preheat the oven to 350°F and line two baking sheets with parchment paper. While the dough is resting, spread the sesame seeds out onto a plate and pour the milk into a shallow bowl.

Cut the dough ball into 4 equal pieces, and roll each piece into ½-inch-thick rope.

Cut each rope into 2-inch-long pieces, then lightly dip each piece in the milk and roll in the sesame seeds until coated.

Place the cookies on the prepared baking sheets about 1 inch apart and bake for 30 minutes until golden.

Allow the regina cookies to cool completely on a wire rack before serving.

Use raw, hulled sesame seeds for this recipe. The seeds do not need to be toasted ahead of time since they're being baked.

If the dough starts to break during rolling, give it a few more minutes. As the dough warms up, it will become more pliable and will hold its shape more readily.

This recipe was written for a conventional oven. For convection ovens, reduce the temperature by 25°F and begin checking for doneness after 22 minutes.

The cookies can be stored at room temperature in an airtight container for 1 to 2 weeks.

PIGNOLI COOKIES

MAKES: 36 COOKIES • PREP: 15 MINUTES • COOK: 15 MINUTES

Pignoli cookies are a classic Sicilian treat that are soft and chewy on the inside and studded with pignoli nuts on the outside. Made with almond paste, sugar, egg whites, and pignoli, these are one of the easiest cookies to make, and eat!

Since pignoli nuts and almond paste are pricier ingredients, bakeries will usually price these cookies at $40 to $55 per pound. Because of this, we always opt to make them at home, especially for the holidays, and we hope that after seeing how easy they are, you'll make them at home too!

INGREDIENTS

1½ cups (210 g) pignoli nuts

1 pound (454 g) almond paste, sliced

1 cup (200 g) granulated sugar

2 large egg whites, at room temperature

¼ cup (28 g) confectioners' sugar, for dusting, optional

INSTRUCTIONS

Preheat the oven to 350°F and line two baking sheets with parchment paper. Lay the pignoli nuts out on a plate and set aside.

Crumble the almond paste into a large bowl or the bowl of a stand mixer fitted with the paddle attachment, then add the granulated sugar and beat on medium speed until combined, about 45 seconds. Add the egg whites and beat on medium until a dough forms, about 2 minutes. The dough will be quite sticky.

Using a cookie scoop, make tablespoon-sized dough balls and roll them between your hands. If needed, dip your hands in water to help prevent sticking.

Roll the balls in the pignoli nuts to coat lightly and transfer to a baking sheet, 1 to 2 inches apart. Using a spoon or the bottom of a glass, press the balls slightly to help the nuts adhere to the cookies, then place in the oven and bake for 15 to 17 minutes. The cookies will be lightly brown but still slightly soft in the center.

Move the cookies to wire racks to cool completely before serving or storing. If desired, sprinkle the cookies with confectioners' sugar.

The pignoli nuts do not need to be toasted ahead of time. The 15-plus minutes they spend in the oven will toast them up perfectly.

The dough is super sticky, so it's recommended that you use a cookie scoop to make it easier to remove the dough from the spoon and create uniformly sized cookies. It's also helpful to keep a small bowl of water nearby to dip your hands into when shaping the cookies.

This recipe was written for a conventional oven. For convection ovens, reduce the temperature by 25°F and begin checking for doneness after 11 minutes.

Pignoli cookies can be stored in an airtight container at room temperature for up to 1 week.

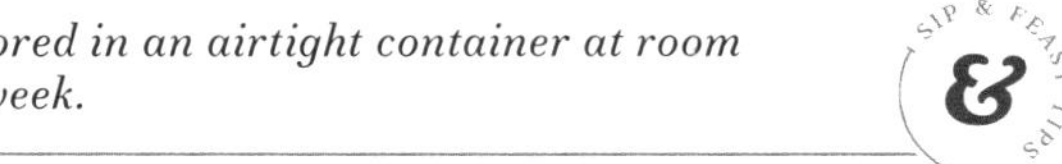

SIP & FEAST TIPS

LEMON RICOTTA COOKIES

MAKES: 48 COOKIES • **PREP:** 30 MINUTES • **COOK:** 14 MINUTES (PER BATCH)

Lemon ricotta cookies are wonderfully airy, loaded with bright lemon flavor, and have just the right amount of sweetness. Topped with a creamy glaze and nonpareil sprinkles, these Italian cookies are always a hit.

We make these every year for Christmas and Easter and they're usually the first to disappear. In fact, Tara always sets aside a separate container for her cousin Michele because she loves them so much. Depending on the holiday, we'll change the color of the nonpareils, and if we make them in the summer, we'll even top them with fresh lemon zest.

FOR THE COOKIES

- 4 cups (520 g) all-purpose flour
- 1 teaspoon baking soda
- 1 teaspoon baking powder
- 1 teaspoon fine sea salt
- 16 tablespoons (226 g) butter, softened to room temperature
- 2 cups (400 g) granulated sugar
- 2 large eggs, at room temperature
- 15 ounces (426 g) whole milk ricotta cheese, drained and at room temperature
- 2 teaspoons vanilla extract
- 2 tablespoons (12 g) lemon zest

FOR THE GLAZE AND DECORATION

- 2 cups (230 g) confectioners' sugar, plus more as needed
- ¼ cup (60 ml) heavy cream, plus more as needed
- 4 tablespoons (56 g) butter, melted
- 1 teaspoon vanilla extract
- 1 pinch salt
- 2 to 3 tablespoons (12 to 24 g) sprinkles, nonpareils, or lemon zest, optional

FOR THE COOKIES

Preheat the oven to 350°F and line two baking sheets with parchment paper.

In a medium bowl combine the flour, baking soda, baking powder, and salt and set aside.

In a large bowl or the bowl of a stand mixer fitted with the paddle attachment, cream the butter and granulated sugar on medium speed, about 2 minutes, scraping down the sides of the bowl if needed.

Add the eggs one at a time and continue to beat on medium until incorporated, then add the ricotta cheese, vanilla, and lemon zest and continue to beat until incorporated.

Begin to add the flour mixture to the ricotta and butter mixture a little at a time while beating on a low speed just until everything is incorporated. Don't overmix. The dough will be sticky and thick.

Using a cookie scoop, drop 1½ tablespoon-sized balls of the dough 2 inches apart onto the lined baking sheets and bake for 12 to 14 minutes or until lightly golden on the edges.

Remove the cookies from the baking sheet and allow them to cool completely on a wire rack before glazing. Repeat for the remaining dough.

FOR THE GLAZE AND DECORATION

In a large bowl, whisk together the confectioners' sugar, cream, melted butter, vanilla, and salt until well combined and smooth. The consistency should not be runny, but should also not be too thick to spread. If the mixture is too loose, add more sugar until you achieve the desired consistency. If it's too thick, add a bit more cream.

Once the cookies have completely cooled, dip the top of each cookie into the glaze and add sprinkles or lemon zest, if desired.

Allow the glaze to firm up on the cookies for at least 2 hours before packing or storing. Refrigerating will speed up the process, if desired.

Depending on which brand you buy, ricotta can be very wet. If the ricotta you are using is very moist, drain it through a cheesecloth or fine-mesh sieve for a few hours to eliminate excess moisture.

The dough can be sticky, so I suggest using a cookie scoop to make the process easier. You can even dunk the scoop in water in between cookies to help reduce the stickiness.

This recipe was written for a conventional oven. For convection ovens, reduce the temperature by 25°F and begin checking for doneness after 9 minutes.

Be sure to add the sprinkles or nonpareils while the glaze is still wet.

Cookies can be stored in an airtight container at room temperature for 3 to 4 days or up to 1 week in the refrigerator. Be sure to let the glaze harden before packing up the cookies for storage.

AFFOGATO

MAKES: 2 SERVINGS • PREP: 10 MINUTES

Affogato is a traditional Italian dessert made with ice cream and coffee, and couldn't be easier! Our recipe calls for vanilla gelato, as its mellow flavor is the perfect background for the intense flavor of the espresso, but feel free to use any ice cream flavor you'd like.

If you own an espresso maker, whether a moka pot or a fancy barista machine, the results will be better than using instant espresso. You can also use strong brewed coffee, or visit a local coffee shop and pick up a few shots of espresso.

INGREDIENTS

4 scoops vanilla gelato

2 ounces (60 ml) warm to hot espresso

Dark chocolate shavings, for sprinkling

INSTRUCTIONS

Place 2 scoops of gelato in each of two small glasses or glass bowls.

Pour the espresso over the gelato, dividing it evenly between the two bowls, and top with the chocolate shavings. Serve immediately.

This is one of those desserts that's easily modifiable. If you want to use more espresso, add it. A drizzle of amaretto or sambuca, a sprinkle of flaky sea salt, or a dollop of whipped cream would also be great!

Serving the affogato in a glass will allow you to sip the remaining liquid after the ice cream has been eaten with a spoon.

BEVERAGES

When we first started Sip and Feast, we envisioned there being an equal number of cocktail recipes to food recipes, but as our path unfolded, we began to focus more on food. While drinks have certainly taken a back seat to the food, we still appreciate the symbiotic relationship a well-crafted cocktail, glass of wine, or pint of beer has with food.

In this section you'll find a few tried-and-true recipes, some of which are already on our website, and some newer ones that are equally delicious. Where appropriate, we'll also suggest ways to make a nonalcoholic version of the drink so there's something for everyone!

WHITE PEACH BELLINI

MAKES: 8 SERVINGS • **PREP:** 5 MINUTES • **CHILL:** 1 HOUR

First crafted in 1948 at Harry's Bar in Venice by Giuseppe Cipriani, the iconic Bellini has become synonymous with Italian aperitivo culture, but here in the United States, and in our home specifically, the Bellini is often served at brunch.

Each year for Mother's Day we host a brunch that usually includes French toast, frittatas, muffins, bacon, scrambled eggs, and more. Tara's stepmom, Angie, usually brings a bottle of prosecco and some peach puree and we enjoy a Bellini or two.

With just two ingredients, peaches and prosecco (plus an optional mint leaf for garnish), the Bellini is hard proof that simple is better—but there is a slight catch. When making any recipe that calls for just a few ingredients, the results will depend heavily on the quality of those ingredients.

For this reason, I suggest using the best peaches you can find, and if that means using frozen because fresh aren't in season, that's perfectly fine. Harry's makes their Bellini with white peaches and that's what we're using here, but you can also use yellow peaches. A good-quality prosecco won't hurt either, but in a pinch you can use any sparkling white wine.

INGREDIENTS

4 large ripe white peaches, plus more slices for garnish

1 (750 ml) bottle prosecco, chilled

1 sprig mint, optional, for garnish

INSTRUCTIONS

Peel and slice the peaches, place them in a bowl, and use a potato masher to mash them, or a food processor to puree them, then place the puree in the refrigerator to chill for at least 1 hour.

Transfer the peach puree to a pitcher, add the prosecco, and mix gently.

Pour into highball glasses or champagne flutes, garnish each with a peach slice and mint leaves, if using, and serve immediately.

SIP & FEAST TIPS

Yellow peaches can be used in place of white peaches; frozen peaches can also be used if peaches are not in season.

To aid in peeling the peaches, cut an X into the bottom of each peach and blanch them in boiling water for 1 minute, then place in an ice bath to cool. Once cool enough to handle, remove the skins.

Use club soda or seltzer in place of prosecco to make nonalcoholic Bellinis.

LIMONCELLO SPRITZ

MAKES: 1 SERVING • **PREP:** 5 MINUTES

When it comes to simple, elegant cocktails, you can't do better than the limoncello spritz. This delightful combination of limoncello, prosecco, and club soda is loaded with bright, sunny flavor and bubbly effervescence, making it perfect for spring and summer.

INGREDIENTS

1 cup (240 g) ice

3 ounces (90 ml) prosecco, chilled

2 ounces (60 ml) limoncello, chilled

1 ounce (30 ml) club soda, chilled, plus more if needed

1 sprig mint, for garnish

3 slices lemon, for garnish

INSTRUCTIONS

Place the ice in a wineglass. Add the prosecco, limoncello, and club soda and give it a gentle stir.

Add the sliced lemon, give the mint leaves a gentle whack on the side of the glass to encourage them to release their oil and aroma, add the mint to the drink, and serve immediately.

Use any herbal garnish you'd like in place of the mint; rosemary, thyme, basil, and culinary lavender would all be great.

Spritzes in general are very forgiving when it comes to ratios, so feel free to adjust the levels as needed. For example, if you prefer a weaker drink, use less prosecco and more club soda.

For a nonalcoholic version, use club soda, lemon juice, and simple syrup to taste in place of the limoncello and prosecco.

HUGO SPRITZ

MAKES: 1 SERVING • **PREP:** 5 MINUTES

Just south of the Austrian border sits the small Alpine town of Naturno, Italy, where the Hugo spritz originated. Inspired by the elder trees native to that area, the original recipe included elderflower syrup, prosecco, and mint.

We've taken a few liberties with our version, swapping out the elderflower syrup for St-Germain or St. Elder (the less expensive version of the elderflower liqueur), and adding some slices of lime. The result is an incredibly refreshing spritz that's perfect for brunches, barbecues, holidays, and even weddings!

INGREDIENTS

1 cup (240 g) ice

6 ounces (180 ml) prosecco, chilled

1 ounce (30 ml) elderflower liqueur, such as St-Germain or St. Elder, chilled

1 ounce (30 ml) club soda, chilled, plus more if needed

3 slices lime, for garnish

1 sprig mint, for garnish

INSTRUCTIONS

Place the ice in a wineglass. Add the prosecco, elderflower liqueur, and club soda and give it a gentle stir.

Add the lime, give the mint leaves a gentle whack on the side of the glass to encourage them to release their oil and aroma, add the mint to the drink, and serve immediately.

Spritzes in general are very forgiving when it comes to ratios, so feel free to adjust the levels as needed. For example, if you prefer a weaker drink, use less prosecco and more club soda.

Use lime-flavored club soda, elderflower syrup, such as Belvoir Farm, and a splash of lemonade for a nonalcoholic version.

ITALIAN SANGRIA

MAKES: 8 SERVINGS • **PREP:** 10 MINUTES • **CHILL:** 1 HOUR

Italian Americans are known for enjoying peaches with wine, whether served as a beverage or as a dessert, *pesche al vino*. This beloved combination inspired this red sangria, which is as easy to drink as it is to make.

It's of course loaded with peaches, but I can't really have a red sangria without apples and oranges, so they've been added too for good measure. I especially enjoy this sangria in the summer alongside anything from the grill, but it is truly great any time of the year, and is perfect for holidays and gatherings.

INGREDIENTS

- 2 large peaches, cubed
- 1 large red apple, cubed
- 1 medium orange, sliced into half-moons
- 2 ounces (60 ml) orange liqueur, such as Gran Gala or Grand Marnier
- 2 ounces (60 ml) brandy
- 2 ounces (60 ml) fresh orange juice
- 1 (750 ml) bottle Italian red wine, such as Chianti, Primitivo, or Sangiovese
- 12 ounces (360 ml) San Pellegrino Aranciata, or other orange soda or seltzer
- 2 cups (480 g) ice

INSTRUCTIONS

In a pitcher, combine the peaches, apples, orange slices, orange liqueur, brandy, and orange juice and allow the mixture to sit for 5 minutes, then add the wine, cover, and place in the refrigerator for at least 1 hour.

Right before serving, add the Aranciata and ice to the pitcher and stir to combine. Pour into glasses and use a spoon to scoop some of the fruit into each glass and serve.

If fresh peaches are not in season, frozen slices can be used.

I like to top off each glass with more Aranciata or seltzer for extra effervescence.

HOLIDAY WHITE SANGRIA

MAKES: 8 SERVINGS • **PREP:** 5 MINUTES • **CHILL:** 1 HOUR

Holiday white sangria originated as our "White Christmas Sangria," but it's so great for other holidays, including Thanksgiving, that we didn't want to limit it to just Christmas!

This one relies on wintry garnishes of rosemary and star anise, which are as aromatic as they are festive, and frozen cranberries for color and to keep the drink cold. Orange slices, whether fresh or dehydrated, add even more texture and color when used for garnish.

Like most sangrias, this one is perfect for holidays and gatherings because it can be made ahead of time and served in a pitcher with a selection of garnishes for guests to help themselves.

INGREDIENTS

2 large Granny Smith apples, sliced

2 dried star anise, plus more for garnish

2 ounces (60 ml) orange liqueur, such as Grand Marnier or Gran Gala

2 ounces (60 ml) brandy

2 ounces (60 ml) fresh orange juice

1 (750 ml) bottle dry white wine

2 cups (200 g) frozen cranberries

16 ounces (480 ml) club soda

Rosemary sprigs, for garnish

Orange slices, for garnish

INSTRUCTIONS

In a large pitcher, combine the apples and star anise with the orange liqueur, brandy, and orange juice and stir to combine.

Add the white wine and stir again. Cover and refrigerate for at least 1 hour.

Right before serving, add the frozen cranberries and club soda and stir.

Add some fruit to each wineglass, then pour in the sangria and garnish each serving with a sprig of rosemary, a star anise, and orange slices. Serve immediately.

Nothing compares to freshly squeezed juice when making cocktails; however, you can use bottled orange juice in a pinch.

Feel free to use flavored sparkling water, such as lime, orange, or cranberry.

Dried orange slices make a beautiful and festive garnish and are a great alternative to fresh slices.

SIP & FEAST TIPS

SACCHETTI SUNRISE

MAKES: 1 SERVING • **PREP:** 10 MINUTES

Situated on Via Sacchetti in Milan, Italy, the Campari Group is the company responsible for one of the all-time greatest spirits, Campari. This bitter liqueur is perhaps most well-known for its use in the Negroni cocktail, but we wanted to use it in a more creative way, and that's how this riff on a tequila sunrise came to be.

In fact, we originally had two versions of the Sacchetti Sunrise, so we asked our Patreon audience to test both versions and let us know which one they liked best. The winner was the frozen blend of peaches, Campari, tequila, grapefruit juice, and orange juice you see pictured here. The other version was equally delicious, but it was not frozen and did not include the peaches (see notes below for the alternate version). A *heartfelt* thank-you to the patrons who tested and shared their feedback on this one!

Because it includes orange and grapefruit juices, the Sacchetti sunrise is great for brunch, but it would be equally wonderful as a pre-dinner drink, especially on a warm summer night.

INGREDIENTS

- ⅓ cup (50 g) frozen peaches
- 2 ounces (60 ml) fresh orange juice
- 2 ounces (60 ml) fresh grapefruit juice
- 1½ ounces (45 ml) blanco tequila
- ½ ounce (15 ml) agave syrup
- 1 to 2 cups (240 to 480 g) ice
- ½ ounce (15 ml) Campari
- 1 orange slice, for garnish

INSTRUCTIONS

In a blender, combine the peaches, orange juice, grapefruit juice, tequila, agave, and 1 cup of the ice and blend until smooth. If a thicker consistency is desired, add another cup of ice and blend again.

Pour the mixture into a rocks glass. Pour the Campari over the back of a spoon onto the top so it disperses over the drink, and give a slight stir.

Garnish with an orange slice and serve.

You may need to adjust the amount of ice depending on your desired consistency.

For an on-the-rocks version without the peach flavor, combine the same amounts of orange juice, grapefruit juice, tequila, and agave in a cocktail shaker, shake vigorously, and pour into a highball glass filled with ice. Pour the Campari over the back of a spoon so it disperses over the drink. Garnish with an orange slice and serve.

For a nonalcoholic version, replace the tequila with more juice (or for the alternate version, with seltzer), and use grenadine syrup in place of the Campari.

THE BEST MANHATTAN

MAKES: 1 SERVING • **PREP:** 5 MINUTES

The Manhattan is as iconic as the city it's named for, and while there are many ways to make a Manhattan, I love this version because it includes a little extra cherry syrup.

Despite my years of living in Manhattan and elsewhere in New York, I'd never actually had a Manhattan until Tara made one for me while we were living in Minnesota. She had picked up Amarena cherries from Trader Joe's and used the cherry syrup to coat the bottom of the glass. I drank it beside the fireplace on a subzero winter night and savored it to the last sip. Since then I've ordered Manhattans in bars and restaurants, but nothing compares to Tara's version, and I truly believe it's the cherry syrup that makes the difference!

INGREDIENTS

2 ounces (60 ml) rye whiskey

1 ounce (30 ml) sweet red vermouth

2 dashes Angostura bitters

1 teaspoon Amarena cherry syrup

3 Amarena cherries, for garnish

INSTRUCTIONS

Fill a cocktail shaker with ice. Add the rye, vermouth, and bitters and shake vigorously.

Pour the Amarena cherry syrup into a coupe glass and tilt and swirl the glass to allow the syrup to coat its interior.

Strain the contents of the cocktail shaker into the glass, garnish with the cherries, and serve immediately.

Traditional Manhattans are made with rye, but you can also use bourbon.

I prefer to use Amarena cherries for their color and taste, but you can use maraschino cherries as well.

The Manhattan is also great served over ice in a rocks glass.

SIP & FEAST TIPS

DIRTY BLOODY MARTINI

MAKES: 1 SERVING • PREP: 5 MINUTES

Tara and I first discovered this riff on a Bloody Mary while on our honeymoon in Aruba. The now-defunct cigar bar Garufa was a favorite spot of ours, and we ended several nights there listening to their piano player and sipping some creative cocktails. Their version of this drink included Clamato juice, vodka, and olive juice. Our version is similar, but we add a few more garnishes for extra flair.

This makes for a great predinner cocktail, but it could also be served for brunch in place of a traditional Bloody Mary.

INGREDIENTS

- 2 ounces (60 ml) Absolut Peppar vodka, or plain vodka
- 1 ounce (30 ml) dry white vermouth
- 2½ ounces (75 ml) Clamato juice or tomato juice
- 1 teaspoon (5 ml) liquid from jarred olives
- 2 dashes Tabasco sauce
- 2 large olives, for garnish
- 1 cube cheddar or other cheese, for garnish
- 1 cornichon, for garnish

INSTRUCTIONS

Fill a cocktail shaker with ice. Add the vodka, vermouth, Clamato juice, olive juice, and Tabasco sauce and shake vigorously.

Strain into a chilled martini glass. Skewer the olives, cheese, and cornichon, place the skewer on the glass for garnish, and serve immediately.

Absolut Peppar is a pepper-flavored vodka with hints of green bell pepper, jalapeño, and black peppercorn, and I love the kick it adds to this drink. Feel free to use any brand of pepper-infused vodka or plain vodka.

Clamato is made by Mott's and includes clam juice, hence its name. If you can't find Clamato, regular tomato juice will do just fine.

Feel free to get creative with your garnishes. Gorgonzola-stuffed olives would be great with this drink!

ESPRESSO MARTINI

MAKES: 1 SERVING • PREP: 5 MINUTES

I first learned how to make an espresso martini from my brother, Greg. He's a renowned bartender on the North Fork of Long Island and makes the most incredible cocktails. This one is no different. While many like to garnish their espresso martinis with coffee beans, Greg always garnishes his with a lemon peel—a nod to the old-school Italian restaurants that would never serve an espresso without a lemon peel.

The espresso martini is great before dinner, but also makes an excellent dessert cocktail, especially alongside a slice of Tiramisu (page 209).

INGREDIENTS

- 2 ounces (60 ml) coffee liqueur, such as Mr. Black
- 1 ounce (30 ml) unflavored vodka
- 1 ounce (30 ml) espresso or strong coffee
- ¼ ounce (7 ml) simple syrup (see notes below)
- 1 lemon peel, for garnish

INSTRUCTIONS

Fill a cocktail shaker with ice. Add the coffee liqueur, vodka, espresso, and simple syrup and shake vigorously.

Strain into a martini or coupe glass, garnish with the lemon peel, and serve. Enjoy!

If you don't have an espresso maker, you can opt for strong black coffee, or you can pick up a few shots of espresso from your local coffee shop.

You can easily make your own simple syrup by combining 1 part sugar and 1 part water and simmering over low heat until the sugar dissolves. Chill in the refrigerator before using.

Mr. Black coffee liqueur uses cold brew coffee and is my preferred brand; however, there are plenty of other options, such as Kahlúa or Tia Maria.

SIP & FEAST TIPS

ACKNOWLEDGMENTS

Writing a book is no small undertaking. It takes time, resources, and the support of others to bring it to fruition. It truly takes a village!

First and foremost, we'd like to thank our children, Samantha and James, to whom this book is dedicated. You've watched *Sip & Feast* evolve from an idea to a full-fledged business and have grown with us along the way. You've dealt with cameras, soft boxes, bright lights, and other equipment taking up space in our home. You've eaten dinner sometimes later than usual so we could get the perfect finished photo. You've taste-tested our food, both on screen and offscreen, never hesitating to give us your honest feedback. You've served as quality assurance experts, sounding boards, idea generators, and so much more. Most of all you've given us our "why," and we couldn't be more thankful for you both.

A huge thank-you to the entire team at Weller Smith Design, especially LeAnna and Erin. Your talent and wisdom brought this book from a mere idea to a work of art, and we could not have done this without you!

A special thank-you to our video editor, Billy Mark. Without your talent and skills we would never have been able to find the time to tackle this cookbook!

A most sincere thank-you to our friend and massively talented photographer Conor Harrigan. Your ability to bring our ideas to life was a joy to watch, and we couldn't be happier with the way everything turned out.

Thank you to Diane DiMartino for answering countless emails and ensuring we have one less thing to worry about.

To our friend Elaina, thank you for planting the "food blog" seed back in 2015. The universe heard you!

Thank you to our readers, Patreon supporters, subscribers, and others who have made *Sip & Feast* what it is today. Your messages, emails, comments, and words of encouragement are what ignited the fire we needed to tackle this cookbook, and we couldn't be more grateful. We especially want to acknowledge the Patreon supporters who have been with us from the very beginning (you know who you are). The fact that you were willing to make a bet on us when we were so small and unpolished really hits hard. You believed in us when were weren't even sure we could believe in ourselves. We appreciate you more than you know.

A special thank-you from Jim:

- To my mom and dad, Fran and Bert, for allowing me to take over your kitchen at an early age and for your continued support through all the years.

- To my brother, Greg, for being my friend, for always believing in me, and for making the best damn espresso martinis on Long Island.
- To my grandma, Mary, for patiently teaching a little kid to cook and for gifting me with the love of cooking. You may not be here on Earth but your legacy will always live on.

A special thank-you from Tara:

- To my mom and dad, Jerry and Linda, for nurturing my love of writing from a young age and for believing in me.
- To my baby sister, Lisa, "Ditto."
- Thank you to my dear friend and fitness guru Dana, for keeping me grounded and giving me a space to clear my head throughout this process and beyond.

And to all our cousins, aunts, uncles, family members, and friends who believed in us right from the start and never hesitated to share our recipes with their friends and network. We are forever grateful.

INDEX

R

S

T

V

W

Z

ISBN: 979-8-9920667-0-8
EBOOK: 979-8-9920667-2-2

Library of Congress Control Number: 2025918158

Designed and Packaged by Weller Smith Design
Lifestyle and food photography by Conor Harrigan on pages: 2, 3, 4, 6, 7, 9, 11, 12, 15, 16, 17, 18, 54, 108, 109, 110, 158, 159, 160, 188, 206, 230, 242, and back cover
All other food photography by James Delmage

Printed in China
10 9 8 7 6 5 4 3
First Edition

Published by Sip and Feast Inc.
Setauket, NY
www.sipandfeast.com